Alienation in Giuseppe Berto's Novels

Scripta Humanistica

Directed by
BRUNO M. DAMIANI
The Catholic University of America

ADVISORY BOARD

Alienation in Giuseppe Berto's Novels

Giacomo Striuli

Scripta humanistica

29

Giacomo Striuli
    Alienation in Giuseppe Berto's Novels.

    (Scripta Humanistica; 29)
    Bibliography: p.
    1. Berto, Giuseppe—Criticism and interpretation.
2. Alienation (Social psychology) in literature.
I. Title. II. Series.
PQ4807.E815Z84   1987   853'.914   86-29769
ISBN 0-916379-30-2

                    Publisher and Distributor:
                    SCRIPTA HUMANISTICA
                    1383 Kersey Lane
                    Potomac, Maryland 20854 U.S.A.

Acknowledgments

I thank all of my teachers, colleagues and friends who have helped and encouraged me in writing this work. I wish to express my gratitude to Providence College, and, personally, to each member of the Committee to Aid Faculty Research, for the financial support that made this work possible. To Bruce Graver and Blossom Kirschenbaum who read the manuscript and gave me useful criticism and suggestions, I am particularly indebted. Finally, I want to thank Maryann Donlon and Gail Philport who generously helped me typing the script. I express my gratitude also to my wife, Nancy, for her patience and support, and finally, to my editor, Bruno Damiani.

a Djella, mia madre.

Contents

Introduction

Giuseppe Berto (1914-1978) is a popular but controversial Italian author whose artistic endeavors include fiction, journalism, playwriting, and cinematography. He published nine novels, three plays, a science fiction "fable," and several short stories. He also wrote the screenplays from some of his novels, which then became successful movies.

Of many writers who have used humor to cope with the absurd, Berto succeeded in both his life and his work. An important Italian literary figure, native of Momigliano Veneto, near Trieste, Berto reveals in his writings the influence of the mittel-european heritage of Freud, Kafka, Svevo and Joyce, what is commonly referred to as the literature of introspection and neurosis.[1]

Despite the commercial popularity of his works, Berto received mixed critical attention and often has been omitted from surveys of contemporary Italian literature.[2] Olga Lombardi, in her valuable monographic study (1974) of Berto, states that he is a most representative contemporary Italian writer:

---

[1] Berto himself in many interviews and in the long prefaces to his works contributed most to the understanding of his life and his artistic endeavors. Critics who have made the most significant contributions to this study are: Olga Lombardi, *Invito alla lettura di Giuseppe Berto* (Milano: Mursia, 1974); Ferruccio Monterosso, *Come leggere Il male oscuro di Giuseppe Berto* (Milano: Mursia, 1977); Corrado Piancastelli, *Giuseppe Berto* (Firenze, La Nuova Italia, 1978); _____, "Berto," *Novecento*, ed. Gianni Grana (Milano: Marzorati, 1979), IX, 7866-86; Giorgio Pullini, *Il romanzo italiano del dopoguerra* (Padova: Marsilio, 1965). Future references to these works will appear parenthetically in the text.

[2] Rossanna Esposito, "Rassegna di studi su Giuseppe Berto," *Critica Letteraria*, 1 (1973), 177-83: "l'assenza di una reale comprensione della sua narrativa, manifestatasi alla apparire del suo primo romanzo, si riscontra anche nella critica successiva."

"Di tutti questi momenti e trapassi Berto è uno dei testimoni più attendibili" (25).

Berto states that his fiction constitutes a "letteratura d'alienazione."[3] Critics, though, tend to minimize this statement. At most, they recognize a dominant concern in Berto for the distorted, neurotic psyches of the characters of his novels, and lament that the author did not equally emphasize the social conditions responsible for their alienation. Berto says: "La critica marxista...mi accusa di aver tralasciato i temi sociali, perchè mi sono sottratto all'alienazione marxista."[4] According to him, existential conviction, alienation is not the result of perverted economics but rather is a malaise pervading contemporary society.

The son of a "maresciallo dei carabinieri," Berto grew up in a climate of fervid idealism and of strict moral principles, devoid of a warm family environment. In 1935 when Berto was twenty-one years old, he joined the fascist army in Ethiopia. Although he was wounded there his valor earned him two medals: "si guadagnò per il suo eroico comportamento in battaglia una medaglia d'argento e una di bronzo al valor militare."[5]

War unveiled to the young idealistic Berto the horrors of the human life. Having been sheltered up until that time in the rose-colored world of patriotism that the fascist regime sought to portray, Berto fell easy victim to the realities of pain, violence, and death in the Ethiopian war. His first-hand experience with pain, which came as the result of wounds suffered in Ethiopia, and his experience as a "camicia nera" fighting in northern Africa, resulted in a psychological shock which caused him to lose his idealism and cast him into the void of doubt and uncertainty. In the following passage, Berto speaks of his shattered ideals: "La grandezza della nazione, la potenza militare italiana, l'unione di tutto un popolo intorno al duce, una finale onestà del fascismo" (IA, 20).

Death became a concrete reality for Berto. The trauma of war and the

---

[3] See Giuseppe Berto, Il brigante (Milano: Rusconi, 1974), p. 9. Future references to this edition will appear parenthetically in the text as BRI.

[4] Claudio Toscani interviews the author in Ragguaglio librario, May 1968, pp. 108-110, quoted in Monterosso, p. 55.

[5] Giuseppe Berto Le Opere di Dio (Roma: Macchia, 1948; in 1965 this work was published by Nuova Accademia, Milano, with the addition of the Inconsapevole approccio, a long and very useful essay in which the author discusses his life, interprets his works and reviews critical appraisals up to the midpoint of his career) p. 18. Future references to this work appear parenthetically as IA (Inconsapevole approccio) or OD (Le opere di Dio).

disillusionment with his political ideals led him to a distorted vision of life and of men. With his typical masochistic honesty the author explains in the *Inconsapevole approccio* the influence of war's ugly experiences on his writings:

> Il senso di colpa del Berto si presenta sotto due aspetti che tenteremo di esaminare separatamente, anche se sono confinanti e spesse volte confusi: il senso di colpa che come uomo egli genericamente sente per le crudeltà della guerra, e il senso di colpa che come italiano e fascista sente per aver contribuito allo scatenarsi della guerra. (*IA*, 30)

Consequently, Berto began to portray alienated lives similar to his own. Realism was his artistic aim, and neorealism became the ideal vehicle to depict the ugly, the painful, and the distorted. In an interview with Giancarlo Vigorelli, Berto states his literary aims:

> ...uno scrittore è davvero utile alla società solo quando realizza se stesso nel modo più completo possibile: anche narrando la vita umana, e questa dovrebbe essere l'aspirazione più giusta per uno che scrive.[6]

As a result of his realistic approach to writing, Berto describes the essential elements of his fiction as being: "frustration, humor, realism, introspection" (*IA*, 16). In his novels, Berto's characters are afflicted with the incapacity to express their innermost feelings; they are lonely people unable to perceive any good in the world. Like Berto himself, these individuals are obsessed with thoughts of pain and death and their own uneasy relationship with God.

According to the neo-Freudian theory of such analysts as Erich Fromm and Karen Horney (see Chapter I), the alienation manifested by the characters of Giuseppe Berto's novels results from the ugly experience of the author's life: the stifling Catholic upbringing, the war, and the disillusionment of his fascist ideals. All of these contributed to the three basic types of alienation found in his works: alienation from God, from self, and from others.[7]

---

[6] See Giancarlo Vigorelli's interview, "Domande a Giuseppe Berto," in *L'Europa letteraria*, No. 27, (March 1964) p. 61. In this important interview the author discusses his literary career, and his interests and aims, dwelling particularly on the *Il cielo è rosso* and *Il male oscuro*. He acknowledges the influence of Freud, existentialism, and of decadentism, especially D'Annunzio. He states that he admires Svevo and Gadda, but does not mention Joyce or Kafka.

[7] Erich Fromm, *The Sane Society* (New York: Holt, Rinehart and Winston,

Berto's literary career can be divided roughly into three phases which reflect three corresponding periods in modern Italian literature: the neo-realism of the 1940s and 1950s, the new avant-garde of the 1960s, and the more conventional literature of the 1970s. The central concern of the first phase of Berto's literary production, alienation from God, is marked by the notion of "male universale," universal evil. In *Il cielo è rosso* (1947), Berto's first major work, he describes the concept of the "male universale": "Oppure avevano maledetto Dio, che era la cosa più giusta, perchè era un modo di maledire se stessi e il male di tutti gli uomini.[8]

The underlying theme of "male universale" is closely related to the theme of guilt. Being alienated from God and taking upon themselves the responsibility for the "male universale." Berto's characters become estranged from themselves and society. As is expressed in the *Inconsapevole approccio*, this condition causes a sense of guilt:

> Berto può cercare incessantemente Dio, ma gli manca l'umiltà per trovarlo, l'umiltà di annullarsi completamente. . . . Un immenso senso di colpa si nasconde pure sotto il titolo *Le opere di Dio*, una bestemmia contro se stessi. (*IA*, 88)

All of the early works, *Il cielo è rosso*, *Le opere di Dio* (1948), and *Il brigante* (1951), were written during Berto's confinement as a prisoner of war at Hereford, Texas, from 1943 to 1946.[9] The protagonists of these novels, respectively Daniele, Filippo Mangano, and Michele Rende, are all victims of the extreme consequences of alienation, insanity and a violent death. Daniele and Michele chose suicide as the ultimate exit from their existential predicament, while the old Filippo aimlessly wanders through the desolate countryside until he is blown up by a field mine.

The development of alienation follows the development of Berto's narrative. With the failure of *Le opere di Dio* and *Il brigante* to achieve critical acclaim, Berto entered a period of virtual silence, and his mental health during the 1950s grew increasingly worse. *Il male oscuro*, however, published in

1955). Fromm's distinction of the three types of alienation is essential to this study. Future quotes from this work will appear parenthetically in the text.

[8] Giuseppe Berto, *Il cielo è rosso* (Milano: Longanesi, 1947), p. 101. Future references to this edition will appear parenthetically in the text as *ICR*.

[9] For a detailed account of Berto's American experience and the critical reception by American critics see *Inconsapevole approccio*, pp. 15-101.

1964, was an instant success. In this highly autobiographical novel, Berto un-ashamedly reveals the most embarrassing truths about his personal life: his doubts as a writer, his fears of sexual inadequacy, and his many phobias. Humor is extremely important in the novel. As the author explains, "humor is the only way I could save myself from insanity," and is a way in which he exposes the "realtà psicologica" of his characters. His major work, *Il male oscuro*, represents the second phase of his literary career and portrays a further stage in the development of alienation, that of alienation from self. As the title itself suggests, the "dark evil", the obscure malady, afflicting the mind of the artist is no longer "universale"; instead, it inhabits the "dark" recesses of Berto's subconscious.

La cosa buffa (1966) and *Oh, Serafina!* (1973) illustrate the third phase of Berto's literary production and the last type of alienation, that of alienation from others. In these novels Berto presents men who are unable to establish happy social relationships because of low self-esteem and hypersensitivity. Antonio, in *La cosa buffa*, and Augusto Secondo, in *Oh, Serafina!*, hesitant-ly approach their sexual partners. Prisoners of their private worlds of fantasy, they are forever caught in the duality of opposite selves and desires.

In addition to describing Berto's existentialism, the notion of alienation symbolizes his vision of life and of art. In fact, Berto believed that "anche nar-rando la propria vita uno può narrare la vita umana." This conviction that he can use his own life as a canvas, against which to project and give life to his characters and stories, emphasizes the link between this notion and Berto's search for selfhood and truth. It also explains Berto's attempt to free himself of a stifling literary past and give credibility to himself as a writer. Berto's dis-trust of his literary peers and his conviction that the artist must integrate his self with his art coincide with Renato Poggioli's description of the artist's isolated role in contemporary society in *The Theory of the Avant-Garde*.[10] For Poggioli, in order to escape the stifling influence of mass culture and, consequently, escape mediocrity, a writer can assert himself only if he aims to break away from others, even at the cost of becoming a "charlatan." He becomes a scapegoat for society's cultural advancement. Only by being ac-cepted as different from ordinary people, he can be useful. Part conqueror and part vanquished, the modern artist is, like Berto, both a clown and a

---

[10] Renato Poggioli, *The Theory of the Avante-Garde*, trans. Fitzgerald (Cam-bridge: Harvard University Press, 1968). Subsequent references to this work will ap-pear parenthetically in the text.

hero. Berto's life and his literary career clearly testify his awareness of his estrangement.

Works such as *Le opere di Dio* (1948) and *Il brigante* had already anticipated the psychological fiction that dominated the 1960s, and with *Il male oscuro* (1966) Berto conveyed his frustration with the formulas of neorealism by stating an alternative strategy, "ora uno scrittore deve guardare il mondo con maggiore distacco, riflessione, senso critico, umorismo." Since, as the author stated, his main preoccupation was to communicate to his readers the "realtà interna" of his characters, his notion of reality comes to coincide with the nonphysical world of psyche. [11] In the 1967's preface to *Il brigante*, Berto criticizes "neorealism" which he denounces as obsolete, frozen in sterotyped formulas, burdened with moralism, and divorced from the needs of the people.

This study discusses his strategies and style as a coherent humanistic philosophy. Each of the major novels will be analyzed, with particular emphasis placed upon the principal characters, plot, setting, and dialogue. However, Berto's recurrent use of both symbols and imagery will also be examined insofar as they serve to reinforce the isolation and estrangement evident throughout the works. Although they are set during very important times in contemporary Italian history, there are not specific time or place references. Feelings seem to supersede historic and concrete actuality.

The characters of these novels also reflect Berto's preoccupation with moral and universal concepts. They are never clearly described. Minute details are seldom provided, but we learn of their most intimate fears and desires. Physical appearance is left to the reader's imagination because Berto's intent is to reveal the inner realty, "la realtà psicologica," of his characters.

The setting also is fixed to traditional and recurrent images of natural phenomena. Rain, fog, and cold are associated with unpleasant and tragic events. Separation and fragmentation are symbolically expressed in the novels by the dualism of the characters (such as in *Il cielo è rosso*, for instance, where the honest and rich Daniele has as his counterpart the petty thief and underworld leader, Tullio) or by the dualism of dark and light. In *Le opere di Dio*, pastoral scenes are ravaged by the destruction of war and the cycle of the seasons is disrupted. Life and death, as well as love and hatred, are frequent extremes in Berto's novels.

---

[11] Aleramo Lanapoppi, "Immanenza e transcendenza nell'opera di Giuseppe Berto: la realtà di dentro," *Modern Language Notes* 1 (1972), 78-104.

Alienation thus marks Berto's literary production not only thematically but also structurally, and stylistically. While exploring the inner lives of the protagonists, Berto seeks a meaning to human existence. Rather than being a photographic portrayal of reality, the novels focus on feelings and ultimate questions. Consequently, Berto cannot be considered an objective writer. Because of his subjectivity, a sense of logical sequence to his works cannot be discerned. We are presented instead with a constantly fluctuating world, one in which there is no stability and which evolves in a pattern of opposite extremes. Yet alienation is his central concern, and it is with an examination of this concept that this study must begin.

I
Alienation

Critics as well as psychologists, sociologists, and novelists agree that alienation can be identified as the prevailing condition of contemporary men. Gerald Sykes calls alienation the "cultural climate of our times."[1] William Bier poses the question, "Alienation: Plight of Modern Man?"[2] For Harold Bloom, contemporary society is the "age of anxiety."[3] The term is used to describe the despair and malaise of contemporary lives, and more specifically, the estrangement of the self.

Alienation thus occupies an important place in many areas of study including economics, political science, philosophy, religion, psychology, psychiatry, sociology, and literature. It is often the central theme of contemporary authors such as Moravia, Bellow, Sartre, Camus, Malamud, and Norman Mailer, who in their writings deal with the search for an identity when they focus on the fragmentation and despersonalization affecting man in today's technological society.

In this regard, however, Alberto Moravia's contribution is helpful because, of all Italian writers, he has utilized the theme of alienation most effectively as the tool for disecting modern society's ills. Moravia's analysis and ap-

---

[1] Gerald Sykes, *Alienation: The Cultural Climate of Our Time* (New York: George Braziller, 1964).

[2] William Bier, *Alienation: Plight of Modern Man?* (New York: Fordham University Press, 1972), p. ix.

[3] Harold Bloom, *The Anxiety of Influence* (New York: Oxford University Press, 1973).

proach in depicting the uglier aspects of life is often disturbing, but, at the same time, his work manifests lucidity and faith in man's capacity for transformation. In *L'uomo come fine* (1964) Moravia gives an interpretation of this elusive word:

> C'è alienazione ogni volta che l'uomo è adoperato come mezzo per raggiungere un fine che non è l'uomo stesso, bensì qualche feticcio che può essere sia il denaro, il successo, il potere, l'efficienza, la produttività e via dicendo . . . . Stando così le cose (l'alienazione ossia la crisi del rapporto con la realtà il fenomeno fondamentale del mondo moderno), non è affatto sorprendente che gli scrittori se ne occupino sia parlandone direttamente nei saggi, sia cercando di rappresentarlo nelle opere di narrativa.[4]

According to Moravia, then, it is a writer's duty to be concerned with the subject of alienation because it negatively affects the lives of all. As seen from the passage cited above, it is the "fenomeno fondamentale" of all contemporary people, resulting from man's loss of his central position in the world.

This approach to reality is manifest also in Berto's writings. Berto's characters are, in fact, cut out from the "realtà esterna," that is, the cultural and social milieu. This failure to relate to the surrounding reality creates a condition of existential despair. As Moravia explains, suffering is the prevailing condition of life for contemporary man:

> ...il dolore dell'uomo moderno nasce precisamente da un senso di profanazione, di sacrilegio, di degradazione che soltanto l'uomo fra tutte le creature è in grado di provare. Di questo dolore è per cosi dire materiato tutto il mondo moderno.... Esso è manifesto in tutte le attività umane, è insomma, l'ordito sul quale è intessuta tutta la trama della civiltà moderna. (238)

In the following passage, Moravia explains how writers can communicate to their readers the causes of alienation in our culture:

> Quali vie seguono gli scrittori per oggettivare l'alienazione, ossia la crisi

---

[4] Alberto Moravia, *L'uomo come fine e altri saggi* (Milano: Bompiani, 1964), p. 377. Subsequent quotes from this edition will appear parenthetically in the text.

del rapporto con la realtà? Due vie, principalmente, quella del realismo e quella dello sperimentalismo. Il primo consiste nella rappresentazione oggettiva e in certo modo scientifica dei fenomeni dell'alienazione in tutti i suoi vari aspetti psicologici e sociali ... lo sperimentalismo si studia invece d'inventare nuove tecniche del linguaggio.... Ma tanto il realismo critico come lo sperimentalismo partono dalla stessa necessità: il carattere oscuro, misterioso, indecifrabile, assurdo della realtà; la mancanza di rapporto con questa realtà; l'alienazione. Ambedue si propongono di ristabilire il rapporto con la realtà; ambedue sentono l'alienazione come il problema centrale del mondo moderno; ambedue infine si preoccupano dell'uomo che essi vedono minacciato nella sua integrità e autenticità. In questo senso bisogna riconoscere che la letteratura contemporanea se non ha ancora risolto il problema, per lo meno lo ha posto in maniera rigorosa e corretta. (380)

There is of course a fundamental ideological difference that divides Moravia from Berto: even if both authors use alienation as a critical perspective from which to view contemporary society, Moravia employs this concept as an ideological marxist framework for his writings. For him, the failure of interpersonal relationships, apathy, the abuse of sex, and the pursuit of materialism are determined by crooked politics, specifically, capitalism. Berto, on the other hand, rejects marxism fearing that "tra marxismo e composizione psicologica umana ci sia un' incompatibilità che costringe il potere alla violenza e alla crudeltà" (*BRI*, 12). Moreover, Moravia maintains a critical distance from his hollow protagonists, while, in contrast Berto seems unable to distance himself from the characters of his novels since he utilizes his personal life as a means to articulate his artistic intent.

Moravia's contributions to the discussion of alienation are most helpful to our understanding of the cultural climate of Berto's writings, but they do not provide a specific definition of the causes and manifestations of alienation. Indeed, it is much easier to describe alienation vaguely as a state of estrangement or separation than to define clearly what it really is. The word is often associated with a large number of psycho-social disorders such as: "loss of self, anxiety states, anomie, despair, depersonalization, rootlessness, apathy, social disorganization, loneliness, atomization, powerlessness, meaningless, isolation, pessimism, and the loss of beliefs or values."[5] The

---

[5] Eric Josephson and Mary Redmer Josephson, "Alienation: Contemporary

variety of applications of the word have virtually rendered it a meaningless term.

Psychological and Social Alienation

Existentialism influenced contemporary psychology and sociology by bringing into focus man's being-in-the-world, the pursuit of freedom and self-determination. Having lost a meaningful relationship with God, the individual faces the hardships of existence alone. As a consequence, he encounters anxiety and frustration. Thus, alienation implies not only the loss of a meaningful relationship with other human beings but also:

> a more basic disturbance of relatedness with both the inanimate structures which constitute one's environment and the historical structures which provide the substance and the continuity of one's experience of self.[6]

The problem of the search for personal identity, the quest of a self, is a major concern today. Neo-psychologists such as Horney, Fromm, and Erikson, in their studies of loneliness, estrangement, and isolation, bring into focus the social and cultural aspects of the individual's life involvement. This is clearly emphasized in an article entitled "An Introduction to the Notion of Alienation," by Ephraim Mizruchi, where he writes that the roots of self-alienation lie in the social system:

> ...social alienation in which individual selves may find the social system in which they live to be oppressive or incompatible with some of their own desires and feel estranged from it.[7]

Psychologists point out that a person cannot have a healthy relationship with others unless he has a healthy relationship with himself. A positive self-image depends primarily on one's family relations during childhood. More-

---

[6] William Meissner, "Alienation in a Psychiatric Perspective," in *Alienation: Plight of Modern Man?* p. 63. Future references to this study will appear parenthetically in the text.

[7] Ephraim M. Mizruchi, "An Introduction to the Notion of Alienation," in *Alienation: Concept, Time, and Meanings*, p. 117.

over, occurrences of great emotional and physical stress may disturb the normal development of an individual's character.[8] In this discussion, we will focus on the thoughts of two neo-Freudians, Fromm and Horney, concerning the psychological state of alienation.

Erich Fromm's lucid account of man's precarious being-in-the-world emphasizes Nietzsche and Kierkegaard's thought:[9]

> In the nineteenth century the problem was that God is dead; in the twentieth century the problem is that man is dead.... The danger of the past was that men became slaves. The danger of the future is that men may become robots. True enough, robots do not rebel. But given man's nature, robots cannot live and remain sane ... they will destroy their world and themselves because they cannot stand ... a meaningful life. (360)

Like the existentialists, Fromm is concerned with the complex problem of achieving a meaningful, productive experience for the individual in modern society. In fact, Fromm draws upon Freudianism and Marxism as well as existentialism in his study of alienation. In his description of modern society, Fromm also shares with Moravia a concern for the dehumanizing qualities of modern life which tend to make robots out of human beings.

Fromm stresses the importance of the individual's healthy relation to the self and to the external world. Still, in *The Sane Society*, he gives this definition of alienation:

> By alienation is meant a mode of experience in which the person experiences himself as an alien. He has become, one might say, estranged from himself. He does not experience himself as the center of his world, as the creator of his own acts—but his acts and their consequences have become his masters, whom he obeys, or whom he may even worship. The alienated person is out of touch with himself as he is out of touch with any other person. He, like the others, are experienced as things are experienced; with the senses and with common

---

8 *See* John A. Clausen, "Social Factors in Mental Illness," *Encyclopedia of Mental Health,* ed. Albert Deutsch (Metuchen, N.J.: Mini Print Co., 1970). Future references to this edition will appear parenthetically in the text.

9 Erich Fromm, *The Sane Society* (New York: Holt, Rinehart and Winston, 1955), p. 360. Future references appear parenthetically in the text.

sense, but at the same time without being related to oneself and to the world outside productively. (120)

Karen Horney sees in alienation a contrast between the real self and the idealized self which results in neurotic behavior.[10] The neurotic hates himself, because he cannot live up to his idealized self. He devalues and torments himself and acts in a self-destructive manner. Moreover, he despises others who present traits and weaknesses similar to his own. Out of touch with the most vital and important part of himself, the individual is separated from his true feelings and needs. His life is empty and tainted with boredom. Meissner summed up Horney's description of the manifestations of self-alienation as follows:

This self-hate expresses itself in relentless demands on oneself, repeated self-accusations, self-devaluation, forms of self-torment, and self-destructive behavior ... more pervasively, alienation can take the form of a feeling of numbness and remoteness. (64)

Thus, the stress placed by Fromm and Horney on experience and external forces as the major causes of self-alienation brings into focus the failure of the individual to relate harmoniously to others. Their observations show clearly that a rigid separation between the psychological and the social cannot be made. Alienation, as Johnson notes, must be considered a "sociopsychic phenomenon" (55). Social factors participate with innate psychological traits in shaping a person's character, or in forming an "alienation syndrome."

The alienation syndrome is the focal point of Meissner's valuable article "Alienation in Psychiatric Perspective":

The elements of the syndrome include a basic sense of loneliness—the feeling that somehow one does not belong, is not a part of things, not in the mainstream of life and interests which surround one. There is a sense of estrangement and chronic frustration. The alienated person carries with him a continual sense of opposition between his desires

---

[10] See Richard Schacht, *Alienation* (Garden City, NY: Doubleday, 1970), pp. 123-153 on Fromm and Horney.

and the wishes and desires of those around him.... He lives in a chronic state of disappointment. (80)

The alienation syndrome is characterized by estrangement from one's cultural and social milieu. Individuals react differently to rejection. They may live in a constant moral vacuum, or they may actively oppose the prevailing values by creating their own. They may be caught up in their own inner conflicts, the result of tension between the partially accepted values of the social and cultural milieu and the values the individual has himself created. Whatever the cause, the ultimate outcome of the alienation syndrome is a depressive condition which includes, besides feelings of loneliness and isolation, feelings of guilt over the failure to live up to one's expectations.

According to Meissner, the essential aspects of the syndrome are "depression, narcissism, and aggression." He concludes his study of alienation by saying:

We have tried to stress the essential dimension of alienation—the disparity between individual and social values, and the rejection and rebellion against social structures. The alienated individual is not merely angry, disappointed, frustrated, and lonely, he is estranged both from the society, in which he lives and from himself. (81)

How can we identify the alienation syndrome in individuals? Frank Johnson delineates six symptoms which he believes indicate a condition of exceptional self-alienation. He points out, however, that his list must be accepted only as "nominal" categories, because human behavior often defies scientific classification. Johnson's symptoms of estrangement are:

1. A tendency to experience exorbitant anxiety and disquietude in relatively ordinary interactions with other people.

2. A tendency toward absorption with ideas and fantasy.

3. An uncertainty at both mental and actional levels of human experience (ambivalence plus hesitation in performance).

4. A gnawing consciousness of lack of "fit" with other individuals or groups.

5. A tendency to retreat and withdraw from others.

6. An alternating vacillation toward and away from social contact. (55)

14

As will be seen, the psychiatric description of the schizoid personality re-markably applies to the alienated behavior of Berto's characters:

This behavior pattern [schizoid personality] manifests shyness, or sen-sitivity, reclusiveness, avoidance of closer competitive relationships, and also eccentricity. Autistic thinking as in daydreaming and the ina-bility to express hostility and ordinary aggressive feelings. These pa-tients react to disturbing experience and conflicts with apparent de-tachment. [11]

As we are about to see in the following chapters, alienation is more than a thematic concern in Berto, it is an integral part of his writing which is re-flected in the structure and style of his novels. From it derives his greatest achievement: his ability of using language to explore and to express the psy-chological recess recesses of his characters, what he calls "la realtà interna." This solicitude for the art of writing fiction is expressed by the concern for ful-filling the demands of form and content and by the desire of integrating his self with his art. Indeed, his life is always the canvas for his artistic aspirations. Having made of his self the locus of his writings, Berto provides the inner structure of his fiction and, thereby, establishes a sense of continuity to his writings.

---

[11] *Diagnostic and Statistical Manual of Mental Disorders*, 2nd. ed. (Washing-ton, D.C.: American Psychiatric Association, 1968), p. 42.

II
Alienation from God

Critics have responded differently to Berto's ambivalent view of religion. Some, like Ferdinando Castelli, see in his works as a "blind fatalistic atheism."[1] Others, like Alfred Hayes, emphasize Berto's amorality.[2] But those who have investigated Berto's fiction more closely, like Corrado Piancastelli, Olga Lombardi, and Donald Heiney, recognize the quest for God as a dominant concern.

Berto himself has repeatedly explained the importance of religion to his narrative fiction. In an interview with Giancarlo Vigorelli, Berto directly links his fiction to his sense of alienation from God. He states:

> Senso di colpa, morte, impotenza dell'uomo di fronte a Dio o al male di vivere sono temi eterni, ne è piena la Bibbia fin dal primo capitolo. Per me la morte di Cristo fu un suicidio, pieno di grandezza e di ostinazione. Sono convinto che Marx ha costruito una colossale trappola per l'uomo pensando di liberarlo.[3]

[1] Ferdinando Castelli, quoted in Olga Lombardi *Giuseppe Berto*, (Milano: Mursia, 1974), p. 115.

[2] Alfred Hayes, "The Works of God," *New York Herald Tribune*, 18 June, 1950, p. 17.

[3] Quoted in Vigorelli, p. 109.

Il cielo è rosso

Although *Il cielo è rosso* (1947) marks Berto's literary debut, it was actually written a few months after *Le opere di Dio*, in 1944. Written at Hereford, Texas while a prisoner of war, this work already contains all the themes and narrative devices that are characteristic of his future novels. Critics today still recognize the literary worth of this first work. Giorgio Pullini states: "*Il cielo è rosso* di Giuseppe Berto, il romanzo più inpegnato e felice del dopoguerra italiano."[4]

In *Inconsapevole approccio* Berto recounts how he was inspired to write this novel. He obtained a copy of *Life* magazine showing pictures of some Italian children feeding themselves on garbage and begging for food. Then, one summer evening, a new group of prisoners from Italy came and told him about the bombing and destruction of Treviso. Berto was inspired and began feverishly to write the book, somehow managing to complete it, as he irreverently tells us, on camp toilet paper (*IA*, 12-13). After the war, Berto presented the book to Comisso and to the publisher Longanesi with the title *La perduta gente*. Not liking the title, Longanesi changed it and published the novel as *Il cielo è rosso* in 1947.

Il cielo è rosso is truly the beginning of Berto's "letteratura d'alienazione". As Corrado Piancastelli states: "i punti fondamentali di Berto: il suicidio, il male universale, il pianto che però non risolve nulla e neppure si trasmuta in fede."[5] The novel tells the story of a group of four young people, two boys and two girls, who must rely on experience and crime to survive in a city (probably Treviso) almost totally destroyed by a massive air raid. But it is not a novel about war; instead, Berto is more concerned with developing complex psychological portraits of the alienation of his main characters. Daniele, the protagonist, is a passive, middle-class sixteen-year-old—"un signorino," as Pancrazi describes him[6]—who has shut himself off from others to protect himself from a dangerous world. Tullio, who dominates the first

---

[4] Giorgio Pullini, *Il romanzo italiano del dopoguerra* (Padova: Marsilio, 1965), p. 179.

[5] See Piancastelli, p. 18, also Lombardi, p. 22 where the critic recognizes the link between the theme of "universal evil" and Berto's mental anguish associated with his loss of a stable concept of self.

[6] Pietro Pancrazi, "Il cielo è rosso," *Scrittori d'oggi* (Bari: Laterza, 1950) p. 83. The critic was the first to praise the young writer by emphasizing his lyrical and psychological description of the reality of war.

half of the novel, is the leader of a band of adolescent thieves, who mixes lofty ideals of brotherly love with hopes for a bloody Communist revolution. Carla is a strong and sensual young woman, Tullio's girlfriend by day and a favorite of American soldiers by night. Giulia, "lunga e magra," is sickly, melancholic, and introverted, a prostitute's daughter who eventually dies of tuberculosis.

The first part of the story introduces the notion of "male universale." The book opens with a grim description of the countryside, the city, and the people who dwell there: "Ognuno era chiuso in sè stesso, e come smarrito, e gli uomini erano divisi, e senza pietà gli uni per gli altri" (*ICR*, 5). It is a scene of devastating isolation, and the isolation of this sordid "città dei morti" prefigures the spiritual isolation and decay of those who dwell there.

Berto first tells of an episode from 1931, when Giulia's mother, a young prostitute, returned home to have her child against the will of her parents. The narrative then skips to the early '40s, when Giulia and Carla are teenagers, living with their grandmother. But an American air raid destroys their city, and their grandmother dies under the rubble. All alone in the devastation, the young girls accept Tullio's offer to live with him in his hide out. From then on, they must live isolated and unseen in the forbidden zone of the "città dei morti."

It is not long before Daniele joins them. He is first seen as a schoolboy, accompanied by a priest as he searches the ruins for the bodies of his parents. His father, a high-ranking state employee, and his mother were buried under the rubble of the skyscraper in which they lived, and Daniele must identify their bodies. The boy seems untouched by what he sees; his demeanor is unaffected; he is almost indifferent. His indifference is extremely important, for it reveals the extent of his alienation. According to Karen Horney, indifference is a pervasive form of alienation. The individual becomes remote and impersonal, incapable of recognizing his true feelings. This kind of alienation from self, writes Fromm, is the first and direct consequence of having lost God as the center of one's being. Similarly, Daniele is cut off from his feelings—he feels no grief for his parents—nor can he take refuge in the religious consolation offered by the priest. Berto writes:

> "Dove abitavi, tu?" domandò di nuovo il prete. Il ragazzo questa volta rispose: "Là in fondo," disse, e indicò le rovine del primo grattacielo. Il prete si tolse il cappello e si passò sulla fronte un grande fazzoletto bianco. Quindi si rimise il cappello. "Coraggio, figliolo," disse. "Vedrai che il diavolo non è poi così brutto come si dipinge." Il ragazzo

rimase ancora assorto nel guardare. "E adesso cosa vuoi fare?" domando il prete.

"Andiamo a vedere se si trovano," disse il ragazzo.

"Là in mezzo?" disse il prete accennando con un largo gesto alle file dei morti. "E'orribile, figliolo. Ti senti abbastanza forte?"

"Sì, signore," disse il ragazzo. E subito si diresse verso le file delle donne morte, e il prete lo seguì da vicino, ma senza voglia. (*ICR*, 95)

The priest goes on to urge the young boy to strengthen his faith and to heed God's will:

"E se per caso tu dovessi sentire nel tuo cuore una voce che ti chiama, io ti scongiuro di ascoltarla figliolo, quella voce, e di seguire la via che ti indicherà il signore, perchè solo facendo così potrai raggiungere la felicità e la salvezza eterna. Lo farai vero?". (*ICR*, 96)

But Daniele will not follow the priest's advice. The war, and now the death of his parents, products of what Berto call the "male universale," have alienated him from society, by depriving him of family, from himself, by estranging him from normal feelings of grief, and from God, by destroying his faith. Berto underscores his alienation stylistically by means of the pauses and staccato-like language of the episode, which deliberately distance the reader from the event. Then the author abruptly shifts his focus to people scattered amid the rubble, searching for the remains of their families.

Seven months later, on a cold winter night, Daniele runs away from school and returns to the city. In the silence of the "città dei morti," he encounters Tullio, who takes him to his hideout. Although suffering severe alienation, he desperately needs companionship and affection. Yet the bourgeois Danielle senses that he is very different from the others, who are clearly his social inferiors. Giulia herself sums up these differences very well:

"Devi sapere tutto di noi. La madre di Tullia era una che lavava biancheria per i soldati, e il padre di Tullio era uno che andava in giro a riparare pentole di rame. Questo era il suo mestiere, quando aveva voglia di lavorare. Sono morti tutti e due, la notte del bombardamento. E il padre di Carla era in prigione perchè aveva rubato. Poi scappò e adesso è in giro, fa ancora il lavoro o qualcosa di peggio e la madre di Carla faceva la serva quattro anni fa è andata a Napoli, e non sappiamo più niente di lei. Carla potrebbe scrivere per cercarla, ma non vuole. Forse è stato suo padre a dirle di non scrivere. E siamo tutti così, io e Carla e Tullio. Devi sapere che razza di gente siamo." (*ICR*, 64)

When Daniele first meets the sensual Carla, the two are attracted to each other. But because he is too ashamed to take off his pants to have them mended, she teases him, and her teasing causes him such intense psychological pain that he has an emotional breakdown. Giulia intervenes at this point, and her words clearly articulate Daniele's alienation:

> Carla continuava a ridere, quasi istericamente. "Non ridere così." Disse Giulia pregando. "Non capisci che gli fai male? E' differente da noi".
> (*ICR*, 144)

Later, when Daniele learns about Carla's nightly activities with the American soldiers, he rejects her and focuses his attention on Giulia, who loves him without restraint.

Although Daniele is the protagonist of the novel, the figure of Tullio, leader of an adolescent band of thieves, dominates the first half of the story. Berto places great emphasis on Tullio's Marxist ideals, but Tullio's leftist ideology is hardly convincing because he mixes lofty ideals of brotherly love with hopes for a Communist revolution.

In chapter eight Tullio and Daniele visit an old man and exchange with him their political and philosophical views which serve to indicate Berto's own. From the discussion emerges the differences which divide them. Daniele's naivetè clashes with Tullio's hard and experienced attitude. Tullio dislikes Americans:

> "Qualcosa fanno . . . ma è come niente. Appena arrivati fecero distribuire delle razioni di minestra. Diecimila razioni al giorno, per dieci giorni. E anche a Natale fecero distribuire delle razioni. Ma che serve? La gente non può vivere mangiando solo a Natale. Bisogna che tutto cambi, perchè la gente viva. Bisogna che ci sia lavoro per tutti, e che tutti trovino da mangiare con i soldi che guadagnano lavorando."
> (*ICR*, 240)

Olga Lombardi rightly notes that Tullio's inner strength derives from the direct experiences of human evil and suffering: "la forza viene dalla conoscenza dell'ingiustizia sociale e dalla fiducia in un mondo più giusto in cui egli crede construirà" (39). Tullio's distrust for politics is motivated by faith in the people's fundamental goodness: "è perchè gli uomini che comandano un popolo non sono mai stati i più buoni. Sono i più forti, o più furbi, magari anche i più capaci, ma non sono mai gli uomini più buoni" (ICR, 241).

Tullio dies while attempting to rob food supplies from an American truck. This tragic and sudden event marks the end of the first part of the novel. The final chapters describe Daniele's falling in love with Giulia who resembles him in many ways. Just as Carla was full of life and somewhat abrasive like Tullio, so Giulia is sensitive and gentle like Daniele. Again, this final part of the book is marked by death: Giulia dies of consumption.

After Giulia's death, Daniele can no longer endure his existential misery. A victim of despair, he decides to go away. On a cold night, he boards a coal train going nowhere. As the train runs through the night, Daniele takes off his clothes and lowers himself beneath the wheels of the train. Berto draws a parallel between Daniele's suicide and Christ's sacrifice of mankind. His action of removing his clothes and throwing them into the fields symbolizes the final separation from the world.

At the end of the novel, Carla is the only survivor. Some critics have misunderstood Carla's character and role, describing her as a cheap, unimportant individual.[7] On the contrary, she is strong, sensual and daring. A true survivor, Carla can withstand the hardships of war and life better than any of the protagonists of Il cielo è rosso. Perhaps she, more than Tullio, is Daniele's real alter ego. Tullio displays many traits that are opposite in nature to those of Daniele, but there is little confrontation between the two. Indeed, Carla is more important in bringing Daniele's inner thoughts into focus. In the following quotation, Carla shows her strength of character as she reproaches Daniele:

> "Ma devi essere più forte" disse la ragazza.
> "Bisogna aver forza per stare a questo mondo vedrai che ti capiteranno tante cose ben peggiori di questa." (ICR, 167)

The themes of the book are primarily religious. At the beginning of the novel we read a passage from the Gospel of Matthew (XVI, 2, 4):[8]

---

[7] Pancrazi writes: "questa Carla, senza Tullio, è troppo poca cosa" (316).

[8] On the religious significance of the title of this novel and of Le opere di Dio, namely the insignificance of man before God, see Berto's Inconsapevole approccio pp. 86-87, and Piancastelli's commentary pp. 24-25.

21

Di sera voi dite: tempo bello, perchè il cielo è rosso; al mattino, poi: oggi tempesta, perchè il cielo è rosso cupo. Ipocriti! Voi sapete distinguere gli aspetti del cielo e non sapete conoscere i segni dei tempi! Una generazione malvagia e adultera domanda un segno ma non le sarà dato altro segno che quello di Giona. (ICR, 6)

In this novel, Berto's main character seems to be fixed forever in time just as the moment when Christ cries out: "My God, my God, why has thou forsaken me?" In the *Inconsapevole approccio*, Berto actually calls Daniele, "un povero Cristo . . . tanto dolorante da sentirsi responsabile d'un male che per molti versi sembrava trascendere la capacità umana di fare del male" (IA, 100). There will be, however, no hope of redemption or resurrection for Daniele.

According to Berto, the presence of evil and suffering in the world is inexplicable unless it can be attributed to the cosmic order. For example, the American pilots who are about to discharge their load of death and destruction onto innocent people are not to be held responsible; for Berto, God is.

Eppure un male universale ha dato loro la possibilità di uccidere delle persone sconosciute, cosí simili a loro stessi. Un male tanto grande, per cui essi portano terrore e morte e distruzione senza pensarci, con la coscienza di compiere un dovere. (ICR, 68)

Similarly, the victims of the air raid are not responsible for their own miseries. They can curse God, but their unanswered curses fall upon themselves, and thus a vicious cycle is created. Their failure to understand the reasons or causes of such cosmic injustice generates further pain, guilt, and isolation. They become angry, frustrated, sullen, or indifferent:

Ma ora pareva che avessero capito l'inutilità di maledire e piangere o gridare, e di pregare anche erano tutti di una stanchezza cupa, anche i disperati anche gli indifferenti.... Di tutta quella strage, era rimasta in loro la coscienza che fosse una cosa ingiusta. Anche senza sapere di chi fosse la colpa potevano dire che era una cosa ingiusta. E la coscienza di ciò li liberava dal vincolo delle leggi con Dio e con gli uomini. (ICR, 101-02)

At the end of the novel, Matthew's threat is realized. It is here that Berto clearly establishes the parallel between Daniele and Christ. For Berto, Christ's

22

death was, a suicide. Having exhausted his life potential, Daniele also has nothing to live for:

> Il mondo non aveva rimedio per il male degli uomini, per l'incomprensione e la solitudine e l'indifferenza. Non c'era rimedio, così che uno veniva spinto fuori dagli altri uomini, lontano. E improvisamente seppe quello che gli restava da fare. Era una grande cosa, ma si sentiva abbastanza calmo per essa. (*ICR*, 400)

Like Kierkegaard, the author distinguishes an eternal God, responsible for the evils of the world, from the figure of Christ, who is a temporal presence on earth, victim of divine will.

Berto employs numerous symbols to suggest his character's predicament. For example their hide-out, "la città dei morti," is emblematic of the alienation from God. The barbed wire, the warning sign, the rotting bodies underneath the rubble, and the cardboard-covered windows also represent the characters' isolation and spiritual decay. They live in total darkness within their refuge. They sleep during the day and live at night. Night and darkness are associated with the protagonist's inner experiences of isolation and void. Moreover, light is associated with God, and darkness with Satan; thus physical darkness has come to symbolize spiritual darkness.[9] The hideout then, represents symbolically the estrangement from God of the people who live there.

Associated with the lack of light is the dismal weather, dominated by fog, clouds, and rain. Berto uses weather imagery to emphasize the despair, loneliness, and ennui of his characters. Rain recurs most frequently. It falls constantly on the ruins, soaking the houses and the people a visual reminder of the melancholy of his characters. At the beginning of the novel, the author gives this description of the "quartiere of S. Agnese" where the story is about to unfold:

> E fuori pioveva. Pioveva spesso in quei giorni, perchè era il principio della primavera. I vecchi muri del quartiere di Sant'Agnese per l'umidità s'incrostravano di salnitro. Le acque del fiume scorrevano sempre con poco rumore ma gialle, con forte odore di melma e di muschio,

---

[9] George Ferguson, *Signs and Symbols in Christian Art*. (London: Oxford University Press, 1973), pp. 41-43.

che si sentiva per le strade e perfino dentro le case. (*ICR*, 36)

Like the rotting stench that penetrates the houses, spiritual decay darkly inhabits the hearts of these people. It is a rainy and cold wintry day in September when Daniele died. People didn't notice; they carried on in the "grigiore" and "tristezza" of their lives.

Besides weather imagery, a magnolia tree is one of the novel's dominant symbols. Trees have always played an important role in Christian symbolism. As George Ferguson explains, a tree can be a symbol of either life or death, depending upon whether it is healthy and strong or poorly nourished and withered. According to legend, after the death of Adam the Archangel Michael instructed Eve to plant a branch of the Tree of Knowledge on Adam's grave. From this branch grew the tree that Solomon moved to the Temple garden, which was later fashioned into the cross.[10]

This tree, the tree of death, is recalled by Berto in his use of the magnolia. In the course of the novel, it becomes Daniele's cross. Because Daniele is so clearly linked with Christ, one could argue that this tree, the magnolia, already associated with Giulia's death, suggests the tree from which the cross was made. That the magnolias decorating the dinner table have become a constant reminder of death is confirmed by Carla's words to Daniele when Giulia dies:

> "Potevamo portarle qualche magnolia. Adesso è tardi" disse Carla. "Lo faremo domani."
> "Si" disse Daniele. "Le piacevano tanto le magnolie" (*ICR*, 366).

The magnolia tree marks Daniele's arrival in the "città dei morti." Alone and untouched against the gray of a cold wintry day, the tree grows out of the ruins covering the dead. It is the first thing Daniele sees from his underground hide-out:

> Il cielo era grigio e freddo. L'unica cosa che si vedeva era un albero di magnolia un po' lontano, che spuntava dalle rovine con qualque ramo, dalla parte dove andava il sentiero. (*ICR*, 136)

Berto uses the magnolia tree further to describe the condition of Giulia,

---

[10] Ferguson, p. 39.

who is fatally ill. Her tuberculosis causes her to vomit blood and debilitates her so much that she is forced to spend several days in bed. Giulia is a tall, thin, pale girl. Her paleness can be associated with the whiteness of the magnolia, her favorite flower, to suggest Giulia's, purity and innocence. White, however, is also the color of death.

In chapter XI, the magnolia tree is linked with the image of the sunset, the dying of the day and the ensuing darkness:

> L'albero della magnolia cresceva già fuori dalla zona dei morti, nel cortile dietro la casa del calzolaio. E anche . . . il giorno moriva. (*ICR*, 273)

Similarly, in chapter XII, the whiteness of the magnolia flowers is contrasted with the darkness of night and the dying of the day:

> Moriva la luce del crepuscolo all'orizzonte e sempre più scura si faceva l'aria della cucina. Ormai si vedevano bene solo gli oggetti chiari, e meglio di tutto le magnolie sulla tavola. Erano una macchia chiara a mezz'aria, e forse uno non avrebbe capito che erano magnolie. (*ICR*, 315)

Magnolias make their final appearance in chapter XV, where they help to reinforce Berto's thematic concern. Daniele says goodbye to Maria—a little girl who lived with them—and gives her these last instructions:

> "Adesso dobbiamo salutarci, Maria" egli disse. La bambina lo guardava stupita, senza dir niente.
> "Ti ricordi l'alberto delle magnolie?" domandò Daniele. Ancora la bambina non rispondeva.
> "Le magnolie" disse Daniele. Possibile che non ricordi l'albero delle magnolie che sta nel cortile, dietro di casa tua?"
> Lo so l'albero disse la bambina.
> "Bene" disse Daniele. "Adesso non ha più fiori, perchè l'estate è passata. Ma un altr'anno verrà ancora l'estate, e ci saranno ancora i fiori. Allora tu devi prendere i fiori e portarli qui e metterli nei barattoli con l'acqua, come faceva Giulia." (*ICR*, 368)

Daniele's request acquires a religious significance. The house represents his and Giulia's sepulcher, while the magnolias in the "barattoli" are a funeral offering. Moreover, the use of this symbolism of death in connection with the cycle of seasons, "verrà ancora l'estate," alludes to the cycle of life which leads to death.

These examples have helped to illustrate Berto's symbolic use of natural imagery. Among the various symbols, the magnolia tree has assumed the metaphorical significance of Daniele's cross. This also suggests a profound religious concern for transcendental truth and death. Having told the lives of youths caught in an allegory about man's perilous journey through life in quest of selfhood and of God.

Le opere di Dio

Although *Le opere di Dio* was not published until 1948, it was Berto's first serious literary achievement, actually written a few months before *Il cielo è rosso*. Central to this simple, short, and very touching novel is the notion of the "male universale." Once more, the characters of this work are victims of a cosmic force which generates despair, suffering, and loss of identity.

The thematic concern of estrangement from God is reflected in this work in Berto's use of a quotation from the Gospel of John, Chapter IX, to begin the novel. Asked by the apostles who might have sinned and thus caused the child to be born blind, the child or his parents, Christ replied: "Ne lui nè i suoi genitori hanno peccato, ma era necessario che fossero manifestate in lui le opere di Dio." Berto thus implies that the misfortunes suffered by the characters of this novel are "works of God."

This theme is manifest in the plot, the setting, and the relationships among the characters of *Le opere di Dio*. The story tells of the ordeals of a family of peasants who are forced to abandon their home and fields as the threat of war approaches. In the one short night, we witness total destruction and dispersion of the family.

The main characters of the novel are Filippo Mangano, his wife, whom the narrator significantly refers to as "la madre," their eighteen-year-old daughter Effa, their young son Nino, their daughter-in-law la Rossa (married to Giacomo, who has emigrated to Germany), and their little nephew.

Their story takes place in one night, from sunset to about ten a.m., during the year 1944. The arrival of the American troops in Italy, drives the characters of the story northward. But these concrete facts, the historical reality, are unimportant. What matters most is not the scenario of war in which the story unfolds, but the portrayal of the uprooting of the characters' inner selves.

The book opens with a description of Filippo Mangano, head of the household and protagonist of the story. He is an old man, estranged from himself and from his family. Having lost his sense of dignity and his authority as head of household, he relies on alcohol as his sole source of comfort:

> Anche quella sera il contadino della Riva, che si chiamava Filippo Mangano, finí per essere un po' ubriaco. Questo gli accadeva quasi sempre, e d'altronde sarebbe stato difficile prevedere le cose che avvennero in quella sera a nella notte che seguì. Per Filippo Mangano il giorno era stato come tutti gli altri giorni, con la sola differenza che il suo figlio minore Nino e la Rossa si trovavano fuori casa, nella fattoria del Ceschina. (*OD*, 3)

Filippo Mangano displays the typical traits of the alienated man; to quote Berto, "solitudine, incomprensione, incapacità d'esprimersi, impossibilità di capire dove sia il bene" (*IA*, 98).

> Il vecchio era già mezzo ubriaco, tuttavia improvvisamente percepì la tristezza che pesava su di loro. Una tristezza non uguale perchè aveva solo in modo vago radici nelle vita stessa e poi cause diverse per ciascuno e sconosciute ma che comunque pesava su di loro, su loro due insieme. (*OD*, 56)

The old man's existential despair, "la tristezza," derives from the deepest levels of existence itself; it is a cosmic malaise. Although it assumes different manifestations, its causes are "sconosciute." Only through the notion of the "male universale" can Berto account for the tribulations of mankind, which are beyond human understanding. This focal thematic concern is expressed by Filippo's wife, "la madre":

> Mi pare che tutto sia inutile, che tutto quella che possiamo fare noi nel mondo sia inutile. Ti metti in un posto e lavori per tanti anni e poi viene qualcosa che ti porta via in una notte sola tutto quello che hai fatto in tanti anni. . . . Abbiamo sempre tirato avanti come si poteva, e per tutta la nostra vita abbiamo lavorato sulla terra e abbiamo fatto dei figli. E' stato proprio Dio a comandarci di lavorare e di fare dei figli. E adesso non c'è più niente di quello che abbiamo fatto, e della nostra vita. E

27

anche degli innocenti come questo che ho in braccio dovranno penare e crescere senza casa, e magari senza padre, e non è giusto. (OD, 186-87)

The inspiration to write *Le opere di Dio* came to Berto — as he reminds us in the introductory work *L'inconsapevole approccio* — while he was in a American war camp at Hereford, Texas, in 1944. He defends his novel against those critics who doubted its authenticity and value on the basis that he wrote about a reality of war he neither witnessed nor experienced. In fact, contrary to the widely praised *Il cielo è rosso*, this book was not well received. Critics disliked Berto's plain and "spoken" language and the emphasis on dialogue.[11] Berto recalls: "la pubblicazione in volume de *Le opere di Dio* fu un passo falso" (*IA*, 62). Though a stylistic dependency on the fiction of American authors such as Hemingway has been object of criticism, a closer scrutiny manifests that Berto's emulation of the great American writer entails a philosophical affinity, more than a similar use of language. What unites them is indeed a shared concern for man's struggle against the void, the "na-da" of existence, or in other words the individual's alienated relationship in respect to his own feelings and those of others. This seems to be the correct interpretation of Berto's often quoted statement: ". . . gli americani, più che 'come scrivere', avevano da insegnarci 'cosa scrivere'" (*IA*, 65).

But an examination of the *Le opere di Dio* simple plot betrays a similari-ty with Hemingway's short stories.[12] The book tells the ordeals of a rural family that must leave their land and their possessions to escape the violence of war. In one short night, we witness the total destruction and dispersion of the family. The protagonists are Filippo Mangano, his wife, whom the author significantly refers to as "la madre," "the eighteen-year-old daughter Effa, the

---

[11] Many American critics, most notably, Alfred Kazin, Edward Parone saw in Berto's first works a poor stylistic imitation of "American writers such as Steinbeck, Saroyan and, above all, Hemingway. Among Italian critics Enrico Falqui and Enrico Emanuelli were most vocal on condemning Berto's originality. In the *Inconsapevole approccio*, the author eloquently defends himself from such attacks. Though he claims total independence, he recognizes an affinity in the perception of life with Heming-way, his literary mentor: "gli americani più che 'come scrivere' avevano da insegnarci 'cosa scrievere" (p. 39). For a complete discussion see also Piancastelli, p. 28-31; Lombardi, p. 27. For a bibliography, see Rosanna Esposito, "Rassegna di studi su Giuseppe Berto, *Critica letteraria*, 1 (1973), 177-183.
[12] Ernest Hemingway, *The Short Stories of Ernest Hemingway* (New York: Charles Scribner's Sons, 1938).

young son Nino, the daughter-in-law la Rossa (married to Giacomo, who has emigrated to Germany), and the little nephew. There is then in this novel a classical unity which is reflected in the unity of the action and of time but also in the sense of tragedy that permeates the novel. Even the characters seem to be icons of human suffering, most often referred to by their titles, "la madre," "la figlia," "il vecchio," "la rossa." In this way they seem to acquire the significance of Greek masks. The language itself assumes biblical qualities. [13] In the following example Berto lyrically captures the essence of Filippo's despair, his estrangement from himself and from others which he is unable to overcome: "Il vecchio fissò gli occhi in volto alla figlia, ed erano occhi umidi e luminosi. Lei non gli aveva mai parlato così. Nessuno gli aveva mai parlato così in quella casa. E lui si sentì pieno di un amore immenso, che non si poteva esprimersi" (OD, 79).

Their tribulations take place from sunset to ten a.m. during the spring of 1944 when the American troops arrived. The entry of the American troops into this rural region of Italy drives the characters of the story northward. But these concrete facts, the historical reality are relatively important. What matters most is not the scenario of war in which the story unfolds, but the portrayal of the uprooting of the characters' inner selves.

The book begins with a description of Filippo Mangano who is an old man estranged from himself and from his family. Having lost his sense of dignity and his authority as head of his household, he relies on alcohol as his sole source of comfort: "Anche quella sera il contadino della riva, che si chiamava Filippo Mangano, finì per essere un po' ubriaco. Questo gli accadeva quasi sempre" (OD, 3).

Mangano displays the typical traits of the alienated man as Berto states: ". . .solitudine, incomprensione, incapacità d'esprimersi, impossibilità di capire dove sia il bene" (IA, 98). He lives absorbed in his own thoughts with a distorted and sad view of reality: "Il vecchio . . . percepì le tristezza che pensava su di loro. Una tristezza non uguale perchè aveva solo in modo vago radici nelle vita stessa" (OD, 56). It is evident that his existential despair, "la tristezza," derives from the deepest levels of existence itself. It is a cosmic malaise whose causes, to Filippo, who resembles many paternal figures of later novels, and who is also a projection of the writer's own troubled self, are

---

[13]   See Lombardi, pp. 100-10; also Claudio Marabini in *Gli anni sessanta: narrativa e storia* (Milano: Rizzoli, 1969), p. 13: ". . . il suo vagare alla macchia [Michele in *Il brigante*] ha il biblico sapore."

totally mysterious, "sconosciute." Only through the notion of the "male universale" can Berto account for the tribulations of mankind which are beyond human understanding. This focal thematic concern is expressed by "la madre": "Ti metti in un posto e lavori per tanti anni e poi viene qualcosa che ti porta via in una notte sola tutto quello che hai fatto in tanti anni....Io non capisco perché Dio ci abbia fatti in questo modo" (OD, 186-87). Even if she cannot understand, Filippo's wife is fully cognizant of the presence of evil in the world and is able to accept it. Her stoicism makes her then the better of the two, and also the most outstanding and memorable character of the book. On the contrary, to escape despair, Filippo drunkenly irritates everyone, hinders matters, and is argumentative. In the following passage Berto lyrically captures the despair and foolishness of the old man:

> Il vecchio riuscì a cogliere la nuova pausa. Disse di nuovo:—ohè!—e di nuovo alzò una mano solennemente, e ancora nessuno gli badò. Ma come la Rossa stava per aprir bocca, egli si mise a gridare. —Sacramento! qua tutti parlano e io non capisco niente—. Era molto agitato, e gridava. —Non sono cose da donne, queste. (OD, 33)

Mangano's description suggests that for Berto alienation is a state into which men are born. So it is with Berto's character. Mangano's failure at communicating and understanding emphasizes his being completely deficient in confidence. According to Old Testament doctrine, Filippo's experience is universal. Due to original sin, people became estranged from God. Filippo is keenly aware of his estrangement, but is unable to explain it. Nor does Berto seem to understand that Jesus Christ healed the division between God and humanity. Instead, Christ is for Berto a recurrent symbol of man's having divorced himself from the divine. This is what we read in the L'inconsapevole approccio, where the author draws a parallel between Daniele, the protagonist of Il cielo è rosso, and Christ. According to Berto, Daniele, as a victim of humanity's evil, "il male universale," arrogantly desires to be like Christ who chose to assume the guilt of mankind, "di volersi assumere i peccati degli altri."[14] In fact, during an interview, Berto flatly declares that Christ's death was truly a suicide full of "grandezza e ostinazione." Eventually, Berto's conviction that Christ was a symbol of man's alienated position with God will be the focus of La gloria (1978) which, unfortunately, was published few days

---

[14] Berto is quoted in Piancastelli, p. 4.

after the writer's death.

But unlike Judas' — the protagonist of this last novel who takes pride in his tragic destiny — Filippo's separation from God accentuates his feelings of worthlessness and frustration. He neither desires to improve his relationship with the members of his family nor seeks a more fulfilling way of life. Instead, he adopts a violent, authoritarian manner in order to prevent others from approaching him. Drinking creates a barrier and a shelter which helps him to maintain his distance from others. Thus, alcohol underscores the characters' aloness, their lack of communication, their divorcement from life.

The symbolism of drinking as a means to escape personal failure and pain is visible in other works, such as, *La cosa buffa* (1966, published in English as *Anthony in Love*), and *Oh, Serafina* (1973), in which weak male protagonists seek the protection of strong willed women. Powerless, as all those who choose drinking as an escape and a protection from life are, these men desire in women not a companion but the mythicized "mother" of their childhood. Even if Filippo's personal traits, his drinking and his distorted view of womanhood, are clearly inspired by Hemingway's "burnt-out" heroes, there is a fundamental difference. Filippo in fact confronts life with a different philosophy. He does not attempt to overcome his alienation with himself and the world like Santiago who, in *The Old Man and the Sea* (1952), struggles against "the impossible odds of unconquerable natural forces."[15] He does not rely on courage, strength, and discipline to become a happy and integrated human being. Filippo is, instead, a passive victim of forces coming from within himself that have been determined by his inability to live up to adverse, but possible, existential circumstances.

Having described Filippo, Berto then tells us that the family has gathered to harvest peas. But the serenity of harvesting is disrupted by the roar of the approaching war. As night comes, the sound of guns prompts the family's causes the total destruction of the family. Filippo is killed; Effa, whom he loves so much, runs aways; "la madre" abandons to their destiny la Rossa, Nino, and the little child.

"La madre" has tried desperately to prevent the family's dissolution. She is aware of Filippo and la Rossa's mutual dislike and tries to mediate between

---

[15] Philip Young, *Ernest Hemingway: A Reconsideration* (University Press, Pennsylvania: The Pennsylvania State University Press, 1966), p. 128; see also Carlos Baker, *Hemingway: The Writer As Artist* (Princeton, New Jersey: Princeton University Press, 1963) for a discussion of Santiago as an indomitable Christ-like fiqure.

them. When Filippo dies, she tells la Rossa:

"Beveva . . . . era ingiusto con te, e con tutti. Ma non era lui per sua natura. Le cose l'avevan fatto diventare così. Aveva avuto molti patimenti nell'altra guerra. . . . Solo in questi tempi era un po' cambiato perchè si era fatto vecchio, e poi è capitato anche che Giacomo è andato a finire in Germania, e allora si è perso tutto. Non diceva niente, ma ci pensava di continuo." (*OD*, 221-22)

Filippo clearly manifests clinical signs of alienation which result from the traumatic experiences of his life. He lives absorbed in a private world of fantasy, engrossed in the contemplation of his confused thoughts, out of touch with daily reality. Moreover, this description of Filippo's behavior closely coincides with the author's own statements in *L'inconsapevole approccio* about war as the source of his relentless sense of guilt in his narrative. In her study of Berto's novels, Olga Lombardi links war with Berto's existential pessimism:

il tema della guerra e della sua crudeltà viene qui ad identificarsi con quel senso di colpa da cui l'autore si sente toccato in quanto uomo, portato dagli eventi a dare sofferenza e morte, con quel male universale che è uno dei temi fondamentali dell'opera di Berto. (22)

Berto's style helps to underscore his dim view of the world and of human understanding. His use of dialogue is particularly effective in conveying the absence of communication among the characters. The short, staccato language in their conversations reflects their isolation from each other. For example, the repetition of "disse" and "rispose," which critics pejoratively have described between them. The following conversation illustrates how their personal conflict is translated into a kind of linguistic estrangement, which serves to reinforce the difficulty they have in communicating:

—Cos'era?—domandò la Rossa.
—Bicoda,—disse il ragazzo evasivamente.
—Cosa, bicoda?—domandò la Rossa.
—Caccia a due code,—disse il ragazzo.
—Roba americana. Erano sette, bassi bassi.
—E sparavano?—domandò ancora la Rossa.
—Mah,—disse il ragazzo.—devono aver preso qualche macchina, sul-

la strada. Si vede fumo.

—Qua vicino?—disse il ragazzo, sempre con indifferenza. Dio,—disse la madre.—E' meglio che andiamo via subito, se cominciano di queste cose. Si,—disse la Rossa.—E' meglio far presto. (*OD*, 137)

It is evident in this conversation as well as in other instances throughout the novel a breakdown of logical and grammatical sequence. As the characters' interpersonal relationships become increasingly more strained so do their attempts at verbal communication. The rapid ripostes also create a kind of mechanical rhythm, reminiscent of Hemingway and Beckettian theatre.[16] The mechanical regularity of their fragmented responses is a stylistic technique of using rhythm to distance the reader from the action. Hence Berto is successful in meeting the demands of content and form by means of stark, essential verbal exchanges.

The culmination of the above story is reached in the final last pages of the novel which describe how Filippo is killed. Walking in a drunken stupor, Filippo Mangano inadvertently steps on a mine. A few German soldiers help "La madre" and "la Rossa" to collect the parts of his mutilated body. The circumstances of his death, the total darkness, his dismemberment are symbolic of Filippo's complete alienation.

Unable to find a cemetery, Filippo's family finally decide to bury him on top of a hill near a small abandoned church. "La madre" hesitates because there is no priest to give him the last blessing, but "la Rossa" cynically remarks: "non addolorarti per il prete. . . . Forse non ci bada molto, lui (*OD*, 167). From the top of the hill, during the burial of Filippo, they see a column of smoke rising in the distance. Their house is burning due to the ravages of war. The destruction of the house and the priest abandonment of his church sharply clarify the displacement of the characters from order, from stability and from God, the center of their being. Here, in the final chapter, the novel reaches its climax or, more appropriately, its moral nadir. "La madre" decides to leave the family. Without Filippo, she feels too lonely and hopeless to endure her existential misery. Capable of caring for others but not for herself, she needs a reason to continue living. Her love and altruism convince her to go to Effa which is now her sole interest in life. So the novel concludes with another journey, another quest, without a resolution to the char-

---

[16] For a discussion of alienation and style, see Martin Esslin, *The Theatre of the Absurd* (Harmondsworth: Penguin Books, 1968).

acters' previous plight. In this ending the novel's adherence to neo-realist aesthetics is more evident. The end of the novel is marked by bitterness and hopelessness because "la madre'"s grief, enhanced by the memory of Filippo's cannot be consoled by "la Rossa:" "come ti senti, madre? — domandò la Rossa. — Ti senti meglio? / —Si,— disse la madre, e scosse la testa con sconforto.— Ma non ha capito, Rossa. Non ha capito" (243).

The estrangement from God suffered by the characters in *Le Opere di Dio* appears in the symbolism of their journeys, just as it did in *Il cielo è rosso*. And in both novels, the end is bitterness and hopelessness because the characters must stand alone against the injustice of mysterious and unknown forces.

Il brigante

The first edition of *Il brigante*, written between 1949 and 1950, was published in Italy in 1951 by Einaudi. The novel was immediately translated and published in countries such as Russia, Japan, France, Holland, Portugal, England and the United States, where it received better reviews than in Italy. Emilio Cecchi considered it a "romanzo molto brutto," but *Time* praised it as "one of the most beautiful and tragic novels, truly a short masterpiece."[17] The novel was also made into a film that was a popular, if not a critical, success.

In the preface to the 1964 edition Berto explains his authorial intentions while defending the book from the attacks of critics. According to Berto, the novel represents his serious attempt to write a truly neo-realist work which would have established him in the eyes of the critics as a legitimate writer: "*Il brigante* rappresenta in mio consciente a volenteroso tentativo di entrare, di pieno diritto, in un movimento culturale chiamato 'neo-realismo'" (*BRI*, 6).

Unfortunately, as Berto himself later realized, the popularity of "neorealismo" was then fading. This is probably what caused the book to be received as coolly by the critics. Perhaps one of Berto's most severe detractors has been Enrico Falqui. In a 1952 article, Falqui attacked *Il brigante* on many

---

[17]   Berto cites in *Time* and Cecchi's ridiculing review the preface of *Il brigante*, p. 5. For a discussion of Berto's *Il brigante* in the context of neorealism see Aleramo P. Lanapoppi, "Immanenza e trascendenza nell'opera di Giuseppe Berto: la trappola del Neorealismo," *Modern Language Notes*, 85, 1 (January 1970), 78-104.

counts. [18] He said that the novels structure was uneven, and that the plot and characters were not believable, especially the protagonist, whom he considered weird and bloodthirsty, half apostle and half Satan. Moreover, Falqui strongly criticized Berto for having ignored and faultily represented the social reality that he sought to portray. The illiterate peasants of Southern Italy are made to speak a polished and learned language, free of any trace of dialect. Despite his correct assessment of the novel's flaws as a neo-realistic work, obviously Falqui fails the quality of Berto's fiction, and missed altogether Berto's concern for existential questions.

In the preface of the novel, Berto states that "sia dal punto di vista culturale che da quello politico, il neorealismo fu soprattutto un grosso fenomeno d'alienazione" (*BRI*, 9). This statement sheds light on the thematic focus of the novel and of the other neo-realist works. *Il brigante*, in spite of its political aspects, is essentially a tormented story about friendship and love: it is, says the author, "una storia psicologica" (*BRI*, 13). Thus the aim of the book is not to condemn political corruption and social injustice, but to portray Michele Rende's tragic life and spiritual misery.

Berto introduces this predominant sense of spiritual misery, conflict and suffocation in the scene which opens *Il brigante*. As in his earlier novels, the weather is stormy nor is there a clear sense of either historical time or location. The reader may deduce that the action takes place in a mountainous region of southern Italy at the time of the African campaign, but that is not especially important. Berto is mainly interested in larger, subjective issues, and thus a definite setting is not needed.

The book tells the story of a war veteran, Michele Rende, who is wanted for homicide and who becomes a brigand to escape the law. Although the story is narrated by Nino Savaglio, a young boy of sixteen, the protagonist of the novel is Michele Rende. As the book begins, Nino recalls the events that took place when he was thirteen, three years before the end of the war. He remembers the sunny spring day when Michele returned from Africa to bury his father, a reference to the African campaign which sets the time at 1941. But the lack of date serves to emphasize the sense of dislocation, and center the events of the narrative.

Reminiscent of Berto's own experiences of war in Northern Africa —namely his wounding and the humiliation of defeat and imprison-

---

[18]   Enrico Falqui, "Il brigante," *Novecento letterario* (Firenze: Vallecchi, 1961). Falqui's critical evaluation of Berto's work is constantly negative.

ment—the novel is particularly autobiographical in its portrayal of Michele Rende, the embittered and isolated war veteran. The autobiographical elements are also reflected in the description of the setting —the mountainous region and the rural life—which recalls Berto's childhood in the region of Veneto, a favorite background in Berto's novels.

Il brigante is also the culmination of the first two novels. In the same forbidding atmosphere of death and insanity which results from their separation from God, it portrays in greater depth the family relationships, particularly that of the father-son relationship.

The novel begins with natural description. Following a long period of heavy rain the weather seems to have calmed. On a sunny day Michele Rende finally arrives in town. He is a soldier, an agent of death. He is also an outsider—he comes from a neighboring town—and he comes to bury his father. Thus from the onset, the reader is aware that Michele can only bring destruction and unhappiness to those who will enter into contact with him:

> Ricordo bene quand'egli arrivò la prima volta nel nostro paese: era primavera, poco tempo prima che venisse la Pasqua. Avevamo avuto un inizio di primavera confuso, quell'anno. Già alla fine di gennaio c'erano state delle giornate proprio calde, e così il grano nei campi esposti al sole era cresciuto in fretta, e in fondo alla valle le gemme degli alberi s'erano ingrossate fino a scoppiare. Ma poi durante tutto il mese di febbraio erano sopravvenute delle burrasche, una di seguito all'altra. Il vento aveva cominciato a soffiare da levante portando nuvole scure che non finivano mai, e l'aria che s'infiltrava nella nostra valle era gelata e carica di pioggia. I terreni da semina, che erano costruiti a terrazza contro il pendio della montagna, divennero pesanti e in molti punti franarono. (*BRI*, 15)

As this passage illustrates, the setting here is emblematic of the suffocating atmosphere in which the characters live. Berto again makes a symbolic use of natural imagery—rain, fog, cold, dark clouds—to accentuate the anguish of the characters. Rain is thus the constant reminder of the inner feelings of the protagonists and is always associated with unpleasant or tragic events.

Rain forebodingly anticipates the arrival of Michele Rende. The name of the town is not given, but there are references that indicate its location in southern Italy, references which Berto confirmed in the preface. The small mountainous town—there is no mention of the sea—is located in the heart of the land. The near localities bear Calabro-Sicilian sounding names—Lauza-

36

ra, Santo Stefano, Grupa, Vico, Guarna—and these are some of the names of the inhabitants: Turri, Ricadi, Savaglio, Aprici, Accursi, Fimiani.

The historical times and facts, however, are unimportant; because of this and because the town lacks a name, the sense of estrangement in the novel is increased. The omniscient narrator is Nino, who tells the story retrospectively. When his narration is resumed it is still springtime. On a sunny morning Michele Rende appears in his dusty khaki uniform, tired under his heavy military knapsack, at the gates of town. The welcome of the townspeople is devoid of the warmth which is usually bestowed on a soldier returning home.

Nino's narration is successful in strengthening the sense of isolation and void in the novel. Michele's thoughts, feelings and actions are never disclosed directly; instead they are filtered through Nino's perspective. This indirect perspective increases the distance between the reader and Michele Rende, an alienating effect which underscores his solitude.[19] In the following passage, Nino recounts his first encounter with Michele and gives us a psychological insight into his troubled character:

> Quel giorno egli non era che un soldato che veniva dalla guerra. Ma non era solo la sua divisa da soldato, ne sono sicuro. No, anche allora c'era qualcosa dentro di lui, negli occhi e nella voce si faceva sentire, e nel suo volto duro, con la bocca che pareva tirata a disprezzo. (*BRI*, 78)

Michele befriends Nino, perhaps for suspicious reasons. Michele has in fact a secret affair with a young woman, Giulia Ricadi, who belongs to a well-to-do family, and Nino becomes their go-between. Accepting half-heartedly, the boy realizes that he is being used and that he is jealous of Michele's attentions. In fact, Nino's attraction to Michele may be the result of his latent homosexual tendencies, as Berto himself says, describing Nino's "infatuazione quasi omosessuale per il brigante" (*BRI*, 11). After a fight with an arrogant rich merchant, Natale Aprici, Michele is severely beaten by Aprici's men. Soon after Aprici is found dead. Michele claims as his alibi that he had spent the night with Giulia Ricadi, but she denies he had done so.

Nino's narration resumes several months later, on a rainy autumn even-

---

[19]   On the link between the reader and the text see Umberto Eco, *Semiotics and the Philosophy of Language* (Bloomington: Indiana University Press, 1984).

ing. Autumn is the death of the year; thus time and setting still underscore the central concern of the book. In the meantime the serene country setting has been disrupted and ravaged by the arrival of the war. The town has been bombed, and the retreating German army has brought further destruction to these innocent people. On this rainy evening, while the entire family is gathered around the fire—Nino, his father and mother, and Miliella, Nino's seventeen year old sister—the quiet and peace of the house is suddenly broken by a hard knocking at the door. It is Michele who escaped from prison: Nino gives the following description of the man and, implicitly, of his inner emptiness. We can see that Michele's "disprezzo" and his supercilious manners are the result of the unfortunate experiences of his life:

> Vi era una rigidezza in lui che non si voleva sciogliere neanche da-
> vanti ai nostri sforzi di essere buoni con lui. Pareva quasi che avesse fa-
> stidio di noi. Ma allora, perchè era venuto proprio da noi? Forse erano
> state la malignità e l'ingiustizia degli uomini a ridurlo così, e le soffere-
> nze patite in carcere. (BRI, 69)

Michele's disharmony with the world, can be explained in psychological terms: ". . . insecurity in intimate relationships deriving from disruption or trauma in early family life, . . . entry in the armed forces, parenthood . . . loss of a loved one, failure to achieve a cherished goal, and similar life experiences," writes John Clausen, are some of the causes of severe physical and emotional stress that may provoke a psychic shock in the individual.[20]

Badly wounded in the spirit by the experiences of war and now by his permanence in the penitentiary, Michele is on the verge of insanity. He has become totally estranged from himself and from others. Miliella, who is innocent and pure, falls in love with Michele. Her words to Nino capture the sense of despair and the loneliness of Michele: "Io penso che lui dev'essere così perchè è solo. Se qualcuno gli fosse vicino, non avrebbe più voglia di fare del male" (BRI, 76).

Michele has come to fetch his gun and to take revenge with it on Giulia Ricadi. But Miliella's love will dissuade him that night. At dawn, Michele has already left, leaving behind with Miliella the promise to make her his wife one day.

---

[20] John A. Clausen, "Social Factors in Mental Illness," *Encyclopedia of Mental Health*, ed. Albert Deutsch (Metuchen, N.J.: Mini Print Co., 1970), p. 1919.

One and a half years later, as soon as the war ends, Michele Rende returns. Nino, who is now more mature, "non ero più il ragazzo di prima," sees things more objectively. Despite Michele's assurance that he has been graced by amnesty, "Ho le carte in regola" (*BRI*, 88). Nino is aware that Michele is still a very troubled individual, as this observation reveals: "Davvero non volevo che diventasse triste. Invece era caduto in una specie di tristezza e stava assorto nei suoi pensieri. Mi dispiaceva, sinceramente" (*BRI*, 89).

Michele's reactions correspond closely to Horney's description of the symptoms of alienation. Like the alienated individual he has become remote and withdrawn. Also, Michele's alienated traits coincide with that tendency towards introspection and absorption into a private world of fantasy, characteristic of schizoid behavior. Michele, however, is able to avoid being the victim of his personal worthlessness by becoming involved with the needs of the community. He becomes a leader in the struggles of the peasants against the oppressive landowners.

In this part of the book Berto tackles a variety of political and social issues, but his mixture of Marxism and Catholicism is very unconvincing. Like Tullio in *Il cielo è rosso*, Michele assumes the role of a Christ figure speaking against the capitalistic system. As several critics have argued, the result is at least ludicrous, and Berto's ideological "pastiche" has been benovolently called a sort of "marxismo romantico."[21] But, despite the opinion of critics, Berto's use of Michele as a Christ figure is strikingly analogous to his earlier works. In *Le opere di Dio*, there is an episode where this parallel is most clearly illustrated. In chapter seven, the old man is likened to Moses leading the Jews to the Promised Land:

> E infine il vecchio aveva detto: —Avanti!— con voce solenne come se fosse risorto in lui l'antico spirito dei capi che guidavano le tribù nelle trasmigrazioni dei popoli. E il figlio Nino aveva incitato i buoi più volte, portando il carro dietro la casa e poi sulla carrareccia che conduceva alla strada grande. (*OD*, 93)

This passage parallels Berto's highly lyrical description of Michele Rende's work with the poor and the exploited—his simple life in the arid plains, his passionate effort to educate these people about social oppression—which

---

[21]   See Vincenzo D'Agostino, *Civiltà letteraria del Novecento* (Catanzaro: Edizioni Frama Sud, 1980), p. 149.

39

ultimately reminds one of Christ. In the following passage the similarity between Michele's words and Christ's Sermon on the Mount is evident in the setting, the choice of words, and the elevated, biblical, tone:

Allora Michele Rende parlava. Parlava con amore della nostra terra, piena di mistero e di energie ancora intatte, e della gente semplice e paziente che da secoli soffriva in silenzio aspettando la giustizia e il regno di Dio tra gli uomini. Ed era un'attesa vana perchè li avevano avviliti con una schiavitù di generazioni, li avevano sempre sottomessi e sfruttati, così che pareva che avessero perduto perfino la volontà e la fede, il desiderio di lavorare e di conoscere. (*BRI*, 99)

By creating a parallel between such characters as Michele Rende and religious figures, the author reveals their isolation from God. Because they live in such moral wastelands, real closeness to God is, for them, another impossibility. Thus by making them Christ figures, Berto ironically emphasizes their religious despair.

The landowners decide that the only way to suffocate the revolt of the peasants is to eliminate Michele Rende. Having discovered that Michele is a runaway, that he had never obtained the commutation of his sentence, they have him arrested. Michele, however, is able to escape prison that night following his arrest. In order to protect his freedom and his love for Miliella, Michele chooses to become an outlaw, a brigand. Miliella runs away with him, and they live together for a few months, hidden in the woods. The episode of Michele's and Miliella's simple wedding in the abandoned country church is particularly touching. But the desecrated church seems a symbol of the absence of God's blessing on their union, and an omen of what is to follow.

On a rainy day in October, Giacomo De Luca, paid by the police, betrays them. As the soldiers attack their hide-out, Miliella, who is pregnant, is killed. The immense grief Michele felt at her death drives him totally insane. Howling and running through the forest like a madman, thirsty for blood, he goes after all those he thought responsible for Miliella's death. His need of revenge is unquenchable. He kills Giacomo, his sister, and all the family of Giulia Ricadi, who had been responsible for his first imprisonment:

Ma poi arrivai. Sul limite della discesa avevo la grande valle davanti, perduta nella nebbia, senza luci. Lui doveva averli uccisi tutti, anche i due vecchi, in un solo mucchio davanti al focolare. Forse non tutti

avevano una colpa tanto grande da dover morire, ma lui li aveva uccisi. Come aveva ucciso i Ricadi, tutti. (*BRI*, 93)

The imagery of rain, fog, and cold once again is emblematic of the suffocating atmosphere in which Michele's life is about to end. Michele can no
longer endure the oppressive forces of life. He no longer can control the
events of his existence. He realizes that his actions, or for that matter, the actions of all men, are controlled by a superior will, a will wholly indiffrent to his
despair. His only desire is to strike those who have done him wrong in the
past, now that he has lost completely all his trust in divine justice:

> "Non puoi averli uccisi senza ragione", dissi. "Tu non uccidi senza
> ragione."
> "Che importa", disse. "Non volevo lasciare dei conti indietro."
> "E ancora a causa dell'assassinio di Natale Aprici", dissi. "E così?"
> "Non lo so", disse. "Forse lo saprò prima di morire. Soltanto non
> volevo lasciare dei conti indietro". (*BRI*, 194)

In the following passage Giacomo De Luca—who has betrayed Michele
Rende and is responsible for Miliella's murder—tries to barricade himself in
the house. His locking all doors and windows in the attempt to shut out death
is symbolic of the isolation, separation, and spiritual death manifested by all
the characters of the book. It is also the reflection of Michele's incipient madness:

> Sentii che chiudeva la porta col catenaccio. Voleva chiudere fuori la
> morte, ma non si poteva. La casa restò chiusa, abbandonata nella neb-
> bia. Era una nebbia fredda che scendeva dalla montagna, e tra poco
> sarebbe stato notte. Avevo preso il sentiero verso il paese, ma non an-
> dai avanti. Non avrei saputo che fare ad Acquamelo. Se era veramen-
> te in trappola, ci avrebbero pensato i carabinieri ad ammazzarlo. Pur-
> chè morisse. Passai di nuovo davanti alla casa chiusa. . . . Il vento non
> era regolare. Si faceva sentire un poco e poi moriva. (*BRI*, 182)

Nino, who is relating the events, appropriately observes that, although
he tries, Giacomo is unable to lock out death. Death pursues him into the
house. Metaphorically, this episode can also be interpreted as his own burial,
and the house is his sepulchre. The image of the house with its total darkness, and the prison-like confinement of its brick wall, bring to a climax the

41

sense of seclusion despair with permeates the novel's ending. Also, the prophecy of death—which Michele's return from war for his father's burial symbolized—comes to its fulfillment.

When the "carabinieri" surround Michele they fear his fierce resistance: "Michele Rende avrebbe sparato. Aveva da morire, ma sarebbe morto come un leone" (BRI, 198). In a final moment of truth, Michele attempts desperately to overcome his alienation. He calls for the "appuntato Fimiani," the brave and honest man who became a drunkard because of the humiliation of having let Michele Rende escape from prison. Michele confronts Fimiani in his last show-down, and allows the "carabinieri" to kill him. Thus, Michele returns to Fimiani his dignity and credibility as a police officer by sacrificing his own life:

> ...arrivò vicino alla casa e si termò, in mezzo al vicolo. Allora Michele Rende apparve sulla soglia, col mitra stretto sotto l'ascella. Nessuno poteva sparargli, perchè c'era l'appuntato Fimiani davanti. E non accadeva nulla. Poi nel silenzio si sentì gridare Michele Rende. "Che fai", gridò. "Spara!"
> "Alza le mani!", intimò l'appuntato. "Spara!", gridò ancora Michele Rende, e dal suo mitra partì una raffica che non finiva mai. Allora anche l'appuntato sparò, bastarono pochi colpi. Michele Rende si piegò su se stesso, e cadde e non si mosse più. Allora la gente si mise a correre, per andare a vedere. (BRI, 198-99)

This is the bitter end of the novel. The author does not seem to leave much hope. All the characters meet a tragic end and even those who survive—Nino, for example—still must remember what he experienced. These tragic events will seriously interfere with his maturation into adulthood. Although Corrado Piancastelli writes that the nemesis of the characters is brought about by their personal flaws, he recognizes that "Dio" is responsible "nella misura in cui tutti gli eventi portano in sè quel misterioso influsso di predestinazione che sfugge al controllo ed alla volontà degli uomini."[22]

Il brigante ends the first phase of Berto's literary career. The author then entered a long period of psychological depression during which he abstained from writing. Having lost his sense of identity like the protagonists of his novels, Berto encountered the dread of his inner emptiness. Through the

---

[22] Piancastelli, p. 45.

help of the psychoanalyst Nicola Perroti, however, Berto was able to avoid the extreme consequences of his neurosis. His struggles against madness and suicide are revealed unabashedly in *Il male oscuro*, his most autobiographical novel.[23] Because of its importance, complexity, and length, this long novel requires a careful and thorough investigation. For these reasons *Il male oscuro* will constitute the focus of the following chapter. As the title indicates, the author is no longer directly concerned with the "male universale" but with the "male oscuro" inhabiting the inner recesses of his psyche. For Berto, alienation from God engendered alienation from self.

---

[23] Giuseppe Berto, *Il male oscuro* (Milano: Rizzoli, 1964). Future references will appear parenthetically in the text; see also Ferruccio Monterosso, *Come leggere Il male oscuro*, (Milano: Mursia, 1977).

III
Alienation from Self

Il male oscuro

With the publication of *Il male oscuro*, by Rizzoli in 1964, Berto at last was recognized as an important writer in contemporary Italian literature.[1]

Oscar Handlin reviewing the book published in English as *Incubus* (1966) writes:

> The writing sustains hilariously funny passages ... There is a cine-matographic quality to the book as a whole ... Among modern novels, *Incubus* is most akin to *Ulysses* .... There is one difference, *Ulysses* ends in the great paean of affirmation, *Incubus* in resignation.[2]

A complicated story about a man's life long struggle with his father, sickness, sex, his ambitions as a man and as a writer, *Il male oscuro* is both literally and figuratively the tale of a man's search for selfhood, his long journey into subconsciousness: "inizio il lungo viaggio verso l'inconscio alla scoperta delle oscure radici dei miei presenti malanni" (*MO*, 1923). The protagonist, having displaced God as the center of his being, falls out of harmony with himself and his environment. His quest for an identity, his problems relating

---

[1] See Monterosso, p. 17.

[2] Oscar Handlin, "Incubus," *The Atlantic*, March 1965, pp. 162-64. Handlin likens Berto's novel to Bellow's *Herzog* and Joyce's *Ulysses*.

to society, and his frustrated pursuit of literary glory clearly mirror to Berto's own life and aspirations. Quoting Flaubert, Berto states as the beginning of the novel: "Da quando Flaubert ha detto "Madame Bovary sono io" ognuno capisce che uno scrittore è, sempre, autobiografico" (MO, 1).

The novel, despite the experimental form of the "psychoanalytical style," shows a great similarity in form and content with the earlier neo-realist works. It is possible to recognize beyond the facade of the new "modus narrandi" a thematic continuity and an equal concern for a simple, colloquial, yet lyrical style. Berto's fundamental "realistic" intent as a writer remains unchanged even when his focus shifts from outside reality to the protagonist's inner reality of despair. Berto explains:

> C'è di fondamentale la mia convinzione di non aver abbandonato per niente il realismo. So tuttavia che la realtà vera, quella che conta è la realtà di dentro.[3]

Il male oscuro, like *Il cielo è rosso*, shows the deep influence of Dante's *Divine Comedy*. The novel depicts a Dantesque journey into the inner world of the subconscious. Aleramo Lanapoppi, in his study of Berto's novels, uses the parallel between Berto and Dante to emphasize the author's pessimism. Berto's spiritual journey, however, does not lead to light or redemption; it takes him instead into the darkest recesses of his sickened soul:

> Il male oscuro è la descrizione non del viaggio della certezza ma di questa selva stessa; una fenomenologia del dubbio e dello sconforto. Gli incontri si susseguono nel cammino ma non si sa se siano santi o dannati: perchè è venuta meno la forza ordinatrice di qualsiasi certezza.[4]

Yet, *Il male oscuro* is, like Dante's, an allegory of man's journey to the underworld in search for meaning to existence. Thus Berto is illustrating man's existential predicament how can he make sense out of the nihilistic quality of contemporary life.

The most significant strength of the novel is Berto's capacity to use form

---

[3] Berto is quoted in Alermo P. Lanapoppi, "Immanenza e trascendenza nell'opera di Giuseppe Berto: 2) La realtà di dentro," *Moderno Language Notes*, 87, 1 (January 1972), 81.

[4] Lanapoppi, p. 87.

45

to underscore meaning. To do so, the author employs stream of consciousness, flash-backs, introspection and shifts in point of view. By the elimination
of punctuation and by syntactal and semantical oppositions such as oxymor-
ons, he is able to convey the obsessions and the memories of the protagonist.
That is, Berto is creating what he calls the psychoanalytical style, which he
uses to present the mental phantasmagoria of the protagonist's mind. It is a
first person narration, and Berto uses this technique to heighten the emotional impact of the story by establishing a direct communication between the
protagonist and the reader. Through the stream of memory of the "I", the
narrator obliterates time and space, past merges with present, dream with
reality. Also, the events of the story are always seen through the alienated
perception of the protagonist, and this helps to strengthen the theme of ambiguity and dualism which is central to the novel. As Berto explains in the following, his "psychoanalytical style" is not meant as a mere technical tool but
as a lens through which his characters' essence, the "realtà di dentro," can be
clearly revealed to the reader. Style must capture the true "being" of his characters:

> . . .nella tecnica delle libere associazioni adottate come sistema narrati-
> vo. . . . Dato un pensiero iniziale o un fatto qualsiasi che serva da pun-
> to di partenza, vi si collegano in una disposizione diciamo così lineare e
> in piena libertà altri fatti o riflessioni che devono sgorgare il più auto-
> maticamente possibile dalle profondità dell'essere, senza alcuna obbli-
> gatoria dipendenza dai concetti e le immagini precedenti. . . . La
> libertà riguarda tanto gli argomenti che le parole e l'ordine dell'esposi-
> zione . . . alla scrittura deve corrispondere la cosa scritta, ossia alla for-
> ma deve corrispondere il contenuto, perché si abbia lo stile.[5]

Because the story line follows the recollections of the protagonist as an
old man, it is difficult to establish a precise chronology of events. To facilitate
this task, the narrator, at the beginning of the novel gives the reader a sum-
mary outline of the book. The story of his life can in fact be divided into three
major phases, each marked by a tragic event. The first phase begins with Berto's birth in 1914, a year which, as the author recalls wrily, would have a
catastrophic effect on humanity. Marked by his father's oppression and fasc-

---

[5] Giuseppe Berto is quoted from an interview on *Il resto del Carlino*, 17 May,
1964, in Lanapoppi, pp. 81-82.

ism, this phase ends with his unfortunate experience of war when Berto was in his twenties. The second phase includes a period in which Berto believes himself to be relatively free of the influence of his father and is able to pursue his professional aims in literature and cinema. The third stage is abruptly initiated by his father's sudden and horrible death. It is during this time that the physical and mental symptoms of Berto's guilt become agonizingly evident. He will marry, have a daughter, divorce, and pursue a career as a writer. As he becomes older he must endure phobias, surgery, failure, and isolation as a result of his psychotic condition. Eventually his only comfort and escape remains this diary of his living hell, which he keeps and we read now as a novel.

After having given the scheme of the novel, the narrator begins to tell of the time when, living in Rome, he was suddenly summoned home to his father's deathbed. His father's death will, in fact, recall those painful physical and mental manifestations of self-alienation that characterize his life. The protagonist himself is fully aware of how this tragic event contributes to the development of his "male oscuro," the "dark malaise."

The narrator is about thirty-eight years old when he receives a long distance call from his mother and sister urging him to come right away, his father is about to die. His father now a "carabiniere in pensione," a low ranking office, upon retiring had opened a small haberdashery, precisely at a time, ironically, as Berto remembers, when hats were going out of fashion. Berto's family, "gente di provincia," country folk, clashes with the flamboyant widow he accompanies, "una vedova francese" (though she says she is from Paris, her accent though betrays less sophisticated origins). Pressured by her, Berto decides to leave. The very night that he is on the train back to Rome, his father dies. Berto's guilt begins to sicken him physically and mentally. From this moment his entire life, his marriage, his career, will be consumed in the attempt to rid his conscience of having abandoned his father. In this particular episode Berto humorously confronts his painful identification with the father:

> . . .padre che sei nei cieli e non tu che stai nella tua cassa di noce che m'è costata invano un occhio della testa, vedi quanto sei entrato in me padre terreno se penso ai quattrini anche nei limiti estremi dell'agonia. (MO, 125)

Berto's guilt at having abandoned his father begins to haunt him and sicken his mind. He becomes afflicted with mysterious ailments: he displays symptoms of agoraphobia as well as claustrophobia (see *MO*, Chapter 6), he is constipated and suffers great abdominal and chest pains. Unable to sleep, Berto passes his nights in a cold sweat, remembering his father after surgery with a bloody and horrible growth protruding from his body:

> . . .tumore esteriorizzato là sulla pancia sempre avevo pensato che un cancro doveva essere qualcosa di schifoso ma così schifoso com'era in realtà certo niente avrebbe potuto farmelo pensare, grosso e schifoso e sanguinolento. (*MO*, 30)

He soon discovers that doctors cannot find an explanation for his sickness. Failing to find relief through surgery and drugs Berto seeks the help of a psychoanalyst, who suggests that he keep a diary of his ordeals, which later become the basis for *Il male oscuro*. Berto thus begins compulsively to record all of his thoughts in random fashion, adopting the "psychoanalytical style." Unrestrained by punctuation and syntax, Berto seems to free associate. The author's style then effectively reflects the mental disarry of his narrator.

Seeking relief for his guilt, for the source of his mental anguish, Berto remembers in detail what he considers the most intimate and significant episodes of his existence. The author recalls how his father often ridiculed him because he was sensitive and studious. Ever since he can remember he had been persecuted by feelings of inadequacy: "il senso di inferiorità e di frustazione che lo ha perseguitato fin dalla nascita" (*IA*, 63). He remembers sexual games with "Lucia la sporca," which resulted in feelings of shame and impulses to punish himself, even by committing suicide. Certainly, God, his mother, or his favorite teacher would have never loved him, if they were to discover his secrets.

Berto delves through the memories of his life. He recalls his strict and hypocritical religious upbringing, his mystical tendencies, his years spent in religious institutions away from his family where he studied day and night to qualify for financial aid. Eventually these pressures became too much for him and he ran away from school several times. In his torment Berto remembers also his efforts to establish himself as a writer when he returned to Italy after the war. He recalls with pain his ordeals with publishers and then with unscrupulous producers interested only in making money (See *MO*, 210-11).

Meanwhile he meets an attractive eighteen year old girl, "una deliziosa ragazzetta." Initially her sensual love brings relief to his anguished state. But soon his self-hatred interferes with his understanding of her sincere and total devotion. He mistakes for sexual perversion her natural craving for physical contact. Though they marry, their relationship is constantly afflicted with quarrels and conflicts. Even the birth of a daughter, Michela, does not help to solve their marital problems. Unwilling to compromise on anything, they fight even over what name to give their child.

Even if the reader is told Berto's side of the story, the facts speak for themselves. It is easy to see that living with someone like Berto is nearly impossible, hence the marriage eventually fails. Berto's wife leaves him for a younger and richer man. Paradoxically, Berto's "male oscuro" reaches its peak when he is at the nadir of his existence, alone with a book to write and a family to support. Berto, on the verge of insanity, contemplates suicide: "che conta la vita se ormai perfino la ragazzetta se n'è andata, dicono che i topi se ne vanno dalla nave quando prevendono il naufragio" (*MO*, 126).

As Berto approaches his sixty-first year, his life, his heart, still seem burdened by misgivings and doubts. He is losing his hair and is beginning to resemble his father more and more. He even recognizes his physical and spiritual identification with his father. According to Berto's analyst, this identification is a positive sign. From his point of view, the theraphy has cured Berto of the symptoms of his mental sicknes. He is convinced that he, by identifying with his father, has been able to gain control over his emotions, his guilt and anger. Berto, however, is not totally free of his anguish, for occasionally he is still afflicted with the symptoms of his "dark" malady. Confined to a self-imposed isolation, he has yet to gain in a clear understanding of his inner reality.

One day his daughter, Michela, on a break from school, comes to visit him. She is already in her teens and, as Berto notices, is very much like her mother. Their encounter is brief and few words are spoken. They seem to have little to say to each other. When she leaves, he burns the three chapters of the books he has been painstakingly writing, and burns with them a picture of his father. He then goes to a well to draw water for the night, no longer caring for the literary glory that once was so important to him.

This sullen episode concludes the novel. As the last words purport, the protagonist looks to death for the resolution of his misery. Though he says he has no regrets, sadness and longing for the missed opportunities of his life, the unattainable glory, still affect his mind:

> . . .ora accendo un fuoco e prendo i tre capitoli del capolavoro e li brucio un foglio alla volta ma senza rammarico perchè si sa che ormai la mia gloria non può importare a nessuno, e poi brucio anche le fotografie del padre morto senza guardarle si capisce e anzi voltando la testa

quando vedo la busta accartocciarsi per il calore.... si è fatto tardi ma inaffierò egualmente l'orto e stasera proverò a portare i due bidoni piene come faceva mio padre può darsi che ce la faccia senza versare l'acqua nè Domine, forse è già tempo. (*MO*, 414-15)

As Berto confirms in an interview, the protagonist's identification with his father represents an attempt to find God: "il tentativo di identificazione col padre diventa, ad un certo punto, un processo di identificazione con Dio. Spero che si sentirà, leggendo il mio libro, che dentro c'è un filone religioso."[6]

Alienation from self and from God thus mark the end of *Il male oscuro*. The protagonist is still in search of himself and religious truth. He is unable to communicate with others and lives in the isolation of Capo Vaticano. Even so the burning, the fire, and his last invocation to God suggest a ritual cleansing, or at least his readiness to accept divine judgment. Perhaps Berto's quest for God will be satisfied only in the afterlife.

A closer reading of the novel reveals that the alienation from self manifested by the author/protagonist is deeply rooted in his childhood. It is the result of a stifling and hypocritical Catholic education. One can easily trace its development from familial conflicts through the ugly experiences resulting from Berto's confrontation with life's harsh reality. The oppressive and stifling home environment is responsible for the "il senso di inferiorità e di frustrazione che lo ha perseguitato" throughout his life. As Horney believes, if the individual cannot live up to the idealized self and is constantly between the real self, object of denigration and negation, and an unobtainable ideal self, he becomes neurotic. He then devalues and torments himself in a self destructive way for crimes that often exist only in his imagination: "avevo conosciuto una quantità di sconforto che un bambino non è in grado di sopportare restando bambino" (*MO*, 94).

Berto's family alienates him. He is the only son among many daughters. His father is domineering, violent and uncaring. His mother, submissive and loving, is his only shelter. Burdened by unfair expectations, the young Berto gradually begins to retreat from his family and is unable to compete for his mother's attention. As a grown man, Berto still remembers vividly how viciously he was treated.

His family is also the source for Berto's alienation from others, and in

---

[6] Giuseppe Berto quoted in Monterosso, p. 71.

particular from women. Berto lucidly recalls the episode which caused him to fear sex. One day he walked in the house and inadvertently saw his parents as they were about to make love. The sight of his father's nudity greatly shocked and frightened him: "si sarà trattato di un solo attimo ma io ne ho ricordo come di un tempo lunghissimo" (MO, 89). After this day Berto develops an obsession with sex. He is unable to accept it as a natural act, seeing every physical contact as a manifestation of brutishness. From his sexual inhibitions Berto also derives a misunderstanding of women. Consequently, he is not able to interact physically with women without feeling guilty and ashamed. Incapable of distinguishing between love and lust, he falsely categorizes women into those who are pure and innocent, like his mother, or dirty and sinful, like Lucia la sporca, "filthy Lucy," the neighborhood slut (see MO, 76, 87).

Berto is placed in a boarding school at age nine. There his alienation grows more evident. Seeking to escape the ugly reality in which he lives—he is beaten and forced to eat rotten food, "pane fetente"—he studies "come un matto" and develops an obsessive love for God. He aspires to unite with God, all "light and goodness." His prayers, however, cannot end the physical and psychological abuses he is mercilessly subjected to. Hence he develops a love-hate relationship with God, mixing curses with his prayers. He can neither forgive nor understand God's silence before his sufferings (see MO, 70).

Berto's alienated traits manifest themselves in his perception of society. He feels unfit, rejected and isolated. In this work as well as many interviews, Berto attacks the social system which, he believes, is responsible for his treatment as an outcast. In the following statement for example, Berto asserts his conviction that he has been blacklisted by Italy's cultural mafia, led by Alberto Moravia:

> Oggi in Italia abbiamo una mafia culturale che, con la connivenza di certe forze politiche e la codardia di certe altre, domina le sessioni culturali della radio, della televisione e dei grossi quotidiani, si è infiltrata nelle case editrici, nel teatro e nel cinema, nei premi letterari. [7]

Integral to Mizruchi's definition of social alienation is the idea that the

---

[7]   Berto quoted in Piero Palumbo, "Perchè denuncio la Maraini," Gente, 28 September, 1974, p. 132.

forces of society are in the way of an individual's fulfillment of his desires. As he explains, the conviction that society is "oppressive and incompatible" to personal "desires" not only generates estrangement from others but also may lead to Meissner's description of psychiatric alienation. In the preceding statement Berto clearly manifests the "alienation syndrome." He believes that his values are at odds with those who should respect and appreciate him. Thus, he lives in a state of chronic frustration expecting constantly to be let down and disappointed. Thus estranged from his cultural milieu, Berto is left in a valueless vacuum. Suffering because he has not lived up to the expectations of his society or of his father, Berto is estranged both from society and from himself. He strives to overcome his inner conflicts, yet seems unable to react positively to criticism. He dissents, but not constructively. Instead of fighting to bring about change, he withdraws into an ineffectual way of life. He is afraid to face the world and is afraid to be alone as evidenced by his phobias, agoraphobia and claustrophobia, which torment him even in his dreams (see *MO*, 147-48).

There are two dreams in *Il male oscuro* that most significantly exemplify what has been discussed so far. In the first, Berto sees himself as the speaker before a large audience. He is attacking Federico Fellini and his film, *La dolce vita*, which has recently been released. Fellini, who is among the listeners, openly displays his approval of Berto's scathing attacks. At the end of the lecture, Fellini and the entire celebrity-filled audience rise to applaud Berto. Again, Fellini is the first to congratulate and embrace Berto for his eloquent speech (*MO*, 72).

The second dream takes place in Rossetti's bookstore, hence the appellation "il sogno della libreria Rossetti" (*MO*, 64). Berto now engages in a bitter diatribe before his intellectual peers; but this time his words are met with absolute indifference. Everybody seems to ignore his vehement charges against his contemporaries and in particular against Moravia, who, incidentally, is in the audience. A mysterious artist wearing a black cape seems to attract the attention of the people in the bookstore. He is working at a drawing that elicits great admiration when it is passed around, as if, Berto writes, they had seen a masterpiece such as the *Divine Comedy* for the first time. These dreams are clear signs of Berto's insecurity and isolation from others. Lacking confidence, he releases his inner frustrations in dreams, which also disclose his craving for attention.

Berto's attempt to satisfy his call to glory and his craving for revenge against his critics in the sphere of the imagination can be explained by using Jungian analysis.[8] Certain aspects of Berto's character in *Il male oscuro* fol-

52

low the outlines of the Jungian introverted personality type. Jung postulates that introverts are prone to subjective thinking, a characteristic demonstrated in Berto by the very demands of his profession and accentuated by his inability to complete his novel. Berto's retreat into isolation and egocentricity emerge from the need to preserve an island stronghold against internal change and possible external intrusion. This state of isolated subjectivity leads him to indulge in a dangerous state of fantasy in which "objects possess puissant and terrifying qualities for him—qualities that he cannot consciously discern but imagines through his unconscious perception."[9] As Jung further demonstrates, certain of these fantasies are directly manufactured by the individual and they assume menacing proportions as his subjectivity increases:

> An analysis of the personal unconscious reveals a mass of power fantasies coupled with fear of the object which he himself has forcibly activated, and of which he is often enough the victim. His fear of objects develops into a peculiar kind of cowardliness; he shrinks from making himself or his opinion felt, fearing that this will increase the object's power.[10]

Jung's suggestion that the introverted personality type (alienation from self) is able to create fantasy objects sheds light on the relationship between Berto and others, particularly the father figure. This concept, can be used to examine the father as a product of Berto's own unconscious. Although Aleramo Lanapoppi, Corrado Piancastelli, Ferruccio Monterosso, and the author himself have recognized the father as Berto's alter-ego, none have closely scrutinized this crucial point in psychoanalytical terms. Referring to Jung, Lanapoppi, most closely focuses on Berto's need to project his inner fears on his father, the "fantasy object," in order to protect his idealistic inner self. Lanapoppi says:

> Berto presenta questo bisogno di produrre un capolavoro come un risultato della travagliata lotta con il padre: esso servirà a far vedere che il disprezzo e le calamitose profezie paterne erano fuori luogo, e per-

---

[8]   Lanapoppi also uses Carl G. Jung to explain Berto's personal disatisfaction and his ambivalent pursuit of the "ideal," see pp. 85-86.

[9]   Carl G. Jung, "General Description of the Types," *Psychological Types*, trans. R.F.C. Hull (1920; rpt. Princeton: Princeton University Press, 1971), p. 379.

[10]   Ibid.

metterà al protagonista di riacquistare la sua autonomia. Ma una dia-
bolica forza, il peso invincibile dei traumi dell'infanzia, impedisce che il
progetto si realizzi: la vittoria andrà al padre, e i tre capitoli saranno tri-
stemente distrutti dal loro autore.[11]

In examining the father as Berto's alter ego it is necessary to refer to
Jung's later work, which explores the nature of the conscious and unconscious elements of the human personality. According to Jung, the psyche is
divided into three regions: the ego, the personal unconscious, and the collective unconscious. The ego stores man's conscious elements, while the other
two regions contain all those which lie beneath the rational surface. The personal unconscious derives from the individual experiences, while the collective unconscious is formed by innate and primitive elements shared by all
mankind. Jung warns that man should not ignore his irrational unconscious
personality. Only by boldly confronting these unconscious forces can man
consider himself a civilized and contributing member of society:

> Progress and development are ideals not lightly to be rejected, but they
> lose all meaning if man only arrives at his new state as a fragment of
> himself having left his essential hinterland behind him in the shadow of
> the unconscious, in a state of primitivity or, indeed barbarism. The
> conscious mind, split off from its origins, incapable of realizing the
> meaning of the new state then relapses all too easily into a situation far
> worse than the one from which the innovation was intended to free
> it.[12]

Jung calls the process of assimilation of the unconscious "individuation"
and claims it is necessary for self-unification. Even if the individual may be
unable to comprehend fully the "dark" areas of his unconscious, he will
benefit from the recognition of his irrational instincts. Nevertheless, the scrutiny of the unconscious, as in *Il male oscuro*, shows, remains a perilous and
torturous ordeal requiring great courage.

Jung stresses the dangers implicit in a total descent into the unconscious. This action can result in a perversion of the imagination, for overly ac-

---

[11]   Lanapoppi, p. 86.
[12]   Carl Jung, "The Psychology of the Child Archetype," *The Archetypes and the
Collective Unconscious*, trans. R.F.C. Hull (1940; rpt. Princeton: Princeton University Press, 1959), pp. 174-75.

tivated senses, realization, his struggle coincides with his ambition to assert himself as a writer.

Whereas imagination represents the free world of the unconscious, form represents its opposite, namely order and reason. Berto's success as a writer is hindered by this opposition. He strives to write a novel but his obsession with form stifles his creativity and prevents him from realizing his dreams of literary glory. The following statement reveals this dilemma: "sarebbe la cosa migliore del mondo uscire da questa tremenda sofferenza per mezzo di un controllo serio della fantasia" (*MO*, 137-38).

For Jung, the exploration of the unconscious is a hazardous enterprise which requires courage. However, once recognizing the lower area, man's conscious elements will maintain a certain stronghold in order to prevent a total descent into the abyss of the unconscious. He symbolizes this concept with the image of fishermen, searching for treasures in the deep, who "will keep their standpoing firmly anchored on the earth, and will thus . . . become fishers who catch with hook and net what swims in the water."[13] Although the unconscious areas contain healthy elements for man's conscious, a failure to maintain this rational perspective will result in a total subjection of the ego to the fantasies and hallucinations of the unconscious, ultimately leading to psychosis. In this state of insanity the individual suffers from a division of the self (schizophrenia), and an increasing inability to distinguish between reality and imagination as the senses become increasingly acute.

In the following passage Berto displays alienation from self. During an attack of mental illness, he sees his own brain protruding from his head. He cannot help noting with horror how similar it is to the tumor which was bulging from his father's stomach:

> . . .arrivo a vedere il mio cervello fuori di me con tutte le volute sangui-
> nolenti . . . molto simile . . . ad un cancro estratto alle viscere del padre
> mio, sennonchè questo mio cervelo esteriorizzato non è morte cancro
> è paura di abissi e di tenebre oltre la morte. (*MO*, 269)

Berto thus confronts his sickened self while on his way into the world of the unconscious.

The first stage in the "Individuation Process" must begin with a confron-

---

[13] Carl Jung, "Archetypes of the Collective Unconscious," p. 20.

tation of the self, and this Jung pictures as the individual catching sight of himself in a reflective surface:

> . . .whoever looks into the mirror of the water will see first of all his own face. Whoever goes to himself risks a confrontation with himself. The mirror does not flatter, it faithfully shows whatever looks into it; namely the face we never show to the world because we cover it with the *persona*, the mask of the actor. But the mirror lies behind the mask and shows the true face. [14]

At the beginning of *Il male oscuro* the protagonist catches sight of himself in the mirror by identifying with the main character the novel. The text, fictional reality, becomes the mirror reflecting the image of the author. The novel, then, well represents the interplay between reality and illusion, autobiography and history. The protagonist only mistakes the author, he is therefore only apparently "real"; he is, rather, a "literary construction," independent from the personality of the author. Still, if we accet Jung's interpretation, in order to comprehend reality, we must abandon all rationality and venture into the subjective irrational world of our dreams. Jung warns that such exploration may result in a state of hostility, for since the unconscious gives us the feeling that it is something quite alien, a non-ego, it is quite natural that is should be symbolized by an alien figure." [15] stresses that the individual must resolve this conflict to achieve an important union of opposites.

Several similarities between Berto and his father underscore the connection between their personalities. They are both egocentric individuals who are incapable of understanding and relating to others. Like his father, Berto is domineering and seems to prefer submissive conformers. Their sexual habits are also very similar. For them, sex is not an act of love and communication but an instrument of power and control. Berto lives isolated in his interest for art as his father lives estranged from his family in the world of the military. As Berto grows older he begins also to assume his father's physical appearance. In the last pages of the novel, he writes:

> In questo padre al quale sembro sono indissolubilmente unito non lo

---

[14] Carl Jung, "Archetypes of the Collective Unconscious," p. 4.
[15] Carl Jung, "Concerning Rebirth," *The Archetypes of the Collective Unconscious*, p. 142.

ricerco . . . nella sua tomba bensì nel tempo in cui era mito e poesia, e
. . . ognuno la sua quiete se la cerchi dove pensa di trovarla, pertanto
andrò verso il paese dove alzando una mano si colgono gli aranci che
traboccano dai giardini, così era mio padre, camminava nell'alba pei
sentieri della Conca d'Oro e alzava la mano . . . ma non ho il coraggio
di passarlo, padre non ho coraggio. (MO, 411-12)

Berto's troubled and ambivalent feelings toward his father reverberate
throughout the text. In the following episode Berto describes with ferocious
irony his mixture of relief and torment at the sight of his dead father:

La volta che mio padre morì, io arrivai, naturalmente, tardi, ossia
quando l'avevano già bello e sistemato su uno dei cinque o sei tavoli di
marmo della camera mortuaria, sbarbato di tutto punto, con indosso il
vestito nero da sposo di quarant'anni prima, che era ancora nuovo
fiammante si può dire, un po' perchè mio padre come me del resto era
parsimonioso e si sarebbe messo indosso sempre i vestiti peggiori, e un
po' perchè subito dopo sposato ingrassò parecchio e il vestito non gli
andava più bene, e in realtà per infilarglielo da morto avevano dovuto
scucirlo quasi tutto di dietro, cosa che però non si vedeva molto dato
che giaceva sulla schiena, dignitoso e solenne nella sua definitiva pace,
e a me, che in quel tempo non ero ancora malato con ossessioni di
morte e altre simili, non dispiaceva guardarlo così com'era, trovavo
che come morto era uno dei più bei morti che avessi mai visto, epper-
ciò mi venne in mente di fargli fare le fotografie. (MO, 14)

This passage also serves to illustrate Berto's humor. As was already anticipated humor is the author's way not only to cope with the absurd but, more
importantly, to free himself of neorealism's stifling influence. Berto himself
discussed the importance of humor in a 1964 interview conducted by Giancarlo Vigorelli for L'Europa letteraria. He said that humor is directly linked to
alienation being both the symptom and the remedy of his neurosis: "L'ironia,
unita alla pietà, da l'umorismo . . . l'unica via per liberarmi della nevrosi".[16]
In other interviews and writings, Berto repeats that humor allows him to deal
with the hardships of existence. In a letter to Alberto Bassan, he writes: "E
talvolta io rido per disperazione, perchè l'ironia è la sola forma di comunica-

---

[16] Vigorelli, p. 64.

zione che ci rimane in un mondo assurdo."[17] Ferruccio Monterosso, in his study of *Il male oscuro*, emphasizes this function of humor:

> Ironia che non emerge, nel libro, solo a tratti, ma che serpeggia frequente, anche quando il male oscuro picchia con particolare violenza: essa pare un meccanismo di difesa che ha contribuito a salvare Berto da una definitiva catastrofe.[18]

It is our uncertainty about the author's true intent, or in other words, the protagonist's ambiguity, his ambivalent attitude, that provokes our humor. In reading this passage we are forced constantly to stop and reconsider the intentions of the author/narrator: is he poking fun at his father or at himself? Critically engaged in assessing the conflicting signals in the attempt to decipher the message, we are cajoled into sympathy but soon we must take our distances. In our reading we are easily taken in and then disappointed.[19] Berto's description of his visit to his father lying on his death bed is humorous because it is so unlike what we would expect. There is an incongrous mixture of romanticism and seriousness that brings us to laughter. He arrives "naturalmente" late, Berto seems to apologize to the reader for his delay which on the other hand, we are made to understand, is something to be expected of him. We also laugh because we more or less consciously recognize the feeling of embarrassment of having arrived late at such an important occasion. The description of his father — literally stuffed into the wedding suit of thirty years earlier (it is ripping at the seams and had to be cut from behind) — brings to mind the image of a puppet, of a human size doll. Bergson's mechanical people also reflect this fusion of human and inanimate elements.[20] Humor lies in the perceived fusing of two opposite realities, as here, the defunct and the puppet. In our recognition of this combination of tragic and comic lies what Pirandello's called the "sentimento del contrario,"

---

[17] Berto, quoted in Monterosso, p. 65.
[18] Ibid.
[19] On the semiological aspects of a linguistic communication see J.A. Fodor and J.J. Katz, eds. *The Structure of Language: Readings in the Philosophy of Language* (Englewood Cliffs, N.J.: Prentice Hall, 1964).
[20] Henri Bergson, *Laughter: An Essay on the Meaning of the Comic.* trans. C. Brereton and F. Rothwell (New York: The MacMillan Company); on humor see also John J. Enck, *The Comic in Theory and Practice* (Englewood Cliffs, N.J.: Prentice Hall, 1960); Sigmund Freud *Jokes and Their Relation to the Unconscious*, trans. and ed. J. Strachey, (London: Hogarth, 1973), VIII.

which helps us to unveil the protagonist's inner reality as well as it awakes the reader's conscience.[21]

Berto's stated intent to communicate with other human beings through his writings and, in so doing, to seek an answer to life's riddles reveals a profound respect for humanity. Humor becomes an emblem of the eternal struggle against a hostile and chaotic world. These aims coincide with Bergson's who similarly noted that "laughter appears to stand in need of an echo . . . laughter always implies a kind of secret freemasonry, or even complicity, with other laughters, real or imagined."[22] Berto constantly delves through the memories of his life. He recalls the most embarrassing episodes of his life, starting from his strict but hypocritical upbringing, his mystical tendencies, his craving for self-esteem and self-assertion, "il desiderio di gloria." As in the previous neo-realist works, *Il male oscuro* emphasizes pain, manifested this time not in violent lives but in the protagonist's struggle against an obsessive fear of illness and death.

Il male oscuro displays the enormous range of Berto's humor. It is directed not only against the protagonist of the novel but also against the surrounding world and the cosmos. Even God and the human condition are treated humorously. Because of his oppressive religious education, Berto's humor, however, is primarily focused on his sexual inhibitions. Jacob Levine, writing in the *Scientific American*, explains this connection/relationship: "Sex and aggression are the main themes of humor because they are the primary sources of most human conflicts and tensions."[23] Examples of humorous aggression appear in every page of *Il male oscuro*. In the following, Berto turns against himself by revealing his phobias and by attacking his wife's normal enjoyment of sex:

> . . .però io nonostante le cure mi sento soffocato ed è proprio quel dannato busto con le sue stringhe e stecche che mi dà questa sensazione di soffocamento, devo andare nel retrobottega e togliermelo senza indugio, e così mi è venuta anche la fobia del busto che è una sottospecie io penso della claustrofobia, ventisettemilacinquecento lire buttate al vento, più quelle per la Spolding e l'equipaggiamento completo, quanti soldi spesi male padre mio. (*MO*, 147)

---

[21]   Luigi Pirandello, "L'umorismo," *Saggi, Poesie, Scritti Vari* (Milano: Mondadori, 1960), pp. 121-60.

[22]   Bergson, p. 6.

[23]   Jacob Levine, *Scientific American*, February 1956, p. 31.

In the following episode Berto uses humor to recall his unhappy experiences at the orphanage. Desolate and alone, he sees himself as a Christ-like figure. The identification with Christ is by now a constant motif in his writing:

> . . .e certo senza pretendere di paragonarmi neppure alla lontana col figlio di Dio un po' vittima mi sento anch'io, strano che tra queste monache affaccendate non ci sia quella rompiscatole che prima veniva a fare poco opportune proposte riguardo alla confessione, prima si stava troppo male e una sofferenze esorbitante di solito non vivifica un sentimento religioso magari trascurato anzi invoglia più che altro alla bestemmia non tutti possono essere Gesù sulla croce. (MO, 127)

Berto repeatedly links his sexual inhibitions to his childhood. Still in his old age the protagonist remembers with his early humiliating experiences, in connection with his desire to punish himself with death, and his desire to take revenge against the world. Berto here identifies with Leopardi:

> con nessuno parlo e di giorno sto sempre chiuso in camera a dormire o a pensare o a cercare nelle opere del sommo Leopardi disgrazie paragonabili alle mie, e di notte esco per la compagna e specie quando c'è una grossa luna che sale sulla pianura gelata . . . innamorati, e io non sono poeta nè innamorato, Dio mio non essere innamorato a vent'anni nè poeta ed egualmente traboccare di febbre sconfinata di fare mio il mondo o di morire e preferibilmente morire. (MO, 176)

Berto's concept of humor, emphasizing the perception of a deeper truth — namely the inner world of characters caught in the dualism of contrasting selves — suggests the comparison with Pirandello. Indeed Berto's humor shares with Pirandello's a keen sensibility for the duality of existence, the perception of a darker reality hiding behind the comic mask of laughter. For Pirandello humor is an anti-intellectual and anti-logical phenomenon which manifests itself in those who have become victims of their own delusions and that evokes a sense of compassion in those who can perceive it. In other words, humor derives from the observation of something which is distorted, something that violates the normal, logical appearance of reality. To illustrate this concept, Pirandello gives the example of an old woman who disguises herself as a young girl to win back the love of her younger husband. This incongrous sight generates at first a comical response which, because of one's innate desire to make sense out of chaos and absurdities, gives way to the respondent's "sentimento del contrario", that is, the awareness of its deeper and compassionate truth. It is then the analytical capacity of man, "della riflessione," that allows us to perceive the simultaneous presence of a face who is crying behind its laughing mask.

Most critics and theorists from Aristotle to Henri Bergson would agree with Pirandello that humor is linked to the duplicity and ambiguity of the world and that to be understood it requires the presence of a reader, a spectator or interlocutor. As Wallace Stevens describes the nature of reality in "Connoisseur of Chaos",

> A. A violent order is disorder, and
> B. A great disorder is an order. These two things are one (Pages of illustrations).[24]

Berto's humor reflects man's struggle with existence, or better, his innate desire to build, organize simplify. Indeed, Berto's craving for order and understanding, "l'abituale preoccupazione di dare un ordine rigoroso ai pensieri," permeates the text. This rage for order is, of course, itself absurd.

The protagonist lives absorbed in a private world of fantasy and his obsessive insistence on reasoning, doubting, speculating, and dreaming, suggested by the repetition of verbs such as "penso/mi chiedo/mi domando/dubito," helps to support the theory that Berto's humor is aimed to protect him from a hostile universe and is linked to his awareness of self. Samuel Leacock also notes in *Humor: Its Theory and Technique*, that "humor at its highest is a part of the interpretation of life."[25]

Indeed whatever form it takes, humor is always a celebration of life. It is a reflection of the struggle with entropy that threatens us all with death. The quintessential element of humor that encompasses theories as diverse as Bergson's and Koestler's is this: we laugh at things which portray a universe simultaneously anabolic (ordered) and catabolic (chaotic in the sense of disturbed or confused). Consequently, humor expresses the possibility to view the improbable if not impossible as possible. This is evident in Bergson's mechanical people who reflect both human and inanimate elements or in Freud's view of humor reflecting the struggle between the communicational

---

[24] Wallace Stevens, *The Collected Poems of Wallace Stevens* (New York: Albert A. Knopf, 1978), p. 215.

[25] Stephen Butler Leacock, *Humor: Its Theory and Technique* (London: John Lane the Bodley Head, 1935), p. 5.

element's (the order) and the id's (the chaotic and the distorted) attempts of self assertion. Life is chaotic, and only a few, such as Berto, choose to exploit that insight to the fullest.

From this perspective, the presence of humor is often most striking in the face of adversity, Berto's "rido per disperazione" makes sense. Here Berto shows the influence of Camus whose thought pervades his writings. In *Le Mythe de Sisyphe* Camus tells the story of Sisyphus who, thrown from Hades and condemned to roll forever uphill a huge boulder, is still able to laugh at the gods. Camus demonstrates that "even within the limits of nihilism it is possible to find the means to proceed beyond nihilism.[26] Man's realization that he is helpless and adrift in a hostile universe precipitates humor when strife, competition, and conflict seems to prevail. Feeling himself caught up in a chaotic universe, man is able to strike back and at least momentarily defy chaos. Controlling chaos in this manner he is its temporary master.

Having prevailed by the strength of his own effort, Sisyphus' victory teaches that man can also create his own values and determine his destiny:

> Pour le reste, il se sait le maître de ses jours. A cet instant subtil où l'homme se retourne sur sa vie, Sisyphe revenant vers son rocher, dans ce léger pivotemente, il contemple cette suite d'actions sans lien qui devient son destin, créé par lui, uni sous le regard de sa mémoire et bientôt scellé par sa mort. Ainsi, persuadé de l'origine tout humaine de tout ce qui est humain, aveugle qui désire voir et qui sait que la nuit n'a pas de fin, il est toujours en marche. (168)

But it is in the final words of the work that Camus makes the most important remark. Sisyphus, despite all, is happy. He is unvanquished because he still retains the capacity to be happy and, implicitly, to be amused by the absurdity of the Gods. For Camus, humor also seems to be the remedy to life's pain and ugliness: "La lutte elle même vers les sommets suffit à remplir un coeur d'homme. Il faut imaginer Sisyphe heureux" (168).

Berto, too, believes man must seek to emulate Sisyphus when confronting life's absurdity and uncertainty. If there is a supernatural power, it does not concern itself with the affairs of men. This is what the young Berto real-

---

[26] Albert Camus, *Le Mythe de Sisyphe*, (Paris: Gallimard, 1942), v. Future references to this edition will appear parenthetically in the text.

izes when he runs aimlessly through the desolate countryside, his tears illumi-nated by an indifferent moonlight. This is also the notion of the "male univer-sale" at the roots of his existential pessismism.

Berto's solution to this predicament is rooted in Camus' theories and requires, in the moral uncertainty of a God-less world, an internalization of all values. Man must create new values and morals, and to make them true he must adhere to them. Berto, however, lives in a constant struggle with him-self. Oscillating between opposite states of desire, he is an alienated hero not fully capable of living up to his existential code. Like Sisyphus, however, Ber-to attempts to recover his ethical and existential equilibrium by waging war on life. He uses weapon against both his "male oscuro" and negative social forces. It allows him to maintain a grip on his existence, to preserve his men-tal clarity, to live out a concept of himself and a vision of life. Furthermore, his capacity to laugh at himself and his miseries indicates that he has not ac-quiesced, that he is alive.

Kant in *The Critique of Judgment*, writes: "Voltaire said that heaven has given us two things to compensate us for the miseries of life, hope and sleep. He might have added laughter to the list."[27] While certainly depressing, this view of man as a victim of life sums up most of the human condition: the universe is harsh, and unforgiving. Each of us learns that no one or no thing can be counted on all the time. Yet we are able to transcend the realm of the ordinary and to defy existential miseries through out capacity for laughter.

Philosophically, then, the humor of *Il male oscuro* provides a perfect means for sharing with the reader Berto's sense of omnipresent death, de-struction, and the seeming capriciousness of the universe. His isolation is as-suaged by the knowledge that we are all united in "aloneness." Linguistically, humor, forging as it does opposites, disrupts the normal circuitry of com-munication. Since the set expectations are temporarily disrupted, they can-not be utilized to analyze the outgoing (in the case of the speaker) or incom-ing (in the case of the hearer) signals; hence their hidden significance cannot be understood immediately. Presented with conflicting, simultaneous signals, we are forced to pause and reflect.

As Schopenhauer observed, the level of seriousness is proportional to the level of potential humor.[28] And this clearly, applies to Berto's penchant

---

[27] Immanuel Kant, *The Critique of Judgement*, trans. J.C. Meredith (Oxford: Oxford Press, 1973).

[28] Arthur Shopenhauer, *The World as Will and as Idea*, trans. R.B. Haldane and J. Kemp (London: Kegan Paul, Trench, Trubner & Co.)

for mortuary humor: "trovavo che era uno dei più bei morti che avessi mai visto." From the feeling of dejection contained in the phrase "ossessioni di morte," Berto leaps to an euphoric state which prompts him not to miss the opportunity to capture with a photo the handsome appearance of the dead father, "mi venne in mente di fargli delle fotografie."

From this discussion of *Il male oscuro* emerge the causes and manifestations of alienation. Because the alienated lacks a constructive perspective, he becomes locked into a negative view of life. Though he tries to gain control over his life, the protagonist of the novel is alone, still afflicted by misgivings and doubts. Though he sought to resolve his existential difficulties, he does not seem on the way to recovery. He appears instead to have acquiesced to a life of quiet despair as he prepares for the end. Moreover, humor is a most salient element because it has thematic, stylistic, and narrative functions. Through the manipulation of language by means of "free associations" the author establishes the pattern of relationships that constitute the inner structure of the apparently fragmented narration. Free associations also help to depict the mental phantasmagoria of the protagonist, in such a way as to enable the reader to reconstruct the story of troubled existence. Humor lets him vent agression and cope with despair.

IV
Alienation from Others

Alienation from others is the central concern of the third and last phase of Berto's literary production. In the novels that are about to be examined— *La cosa buffa* (1966), *Oh! Serafina!* (1973), *La gloria* (1978)—Berto presents men who are unable to establish happy social relationships because of low self esteem and hypersensitivity. They have failed to develop close relationships for fear of being belittled or humiliated, and as a result feel frustrated, guilty, and depressed. To seek to escape their painful state of self-doubt and insecurity, they immerse themselves in a private dream world.

The relief that dreaming can bring to such characters as Antonio, Augusto, and Judas is often short-lived because their thoughts ultimately remind them of their pitiful state. Deprived of feelings of self-worth, they lack the strength to overcome their anxieties. Eventually, the inner dream world in which they seek refuge becomes their prison. They live through life vacillating between conflicting, irreconcilable desires and are never in touch with reality. Concerned as they are with their ego, these men are unable to relate to others, especially to the women. In order to protect themselves, they seek only the company of someone who, like their mother, can give them unselfish love and protection.

La cosa buffa

La cosa buffa is about the unfortunate loves of Antonio, his solitude, and his literary ambitions.[1] Published in 1966 in Italy, and in 1968 in the United States under the title of *Antonio in Love*, Berto's novel relies heavily on his preceding works, but shows a more traditional novelistic intent. It is the sequel to *Il male oscuro*, but unlike the earlier novel, is a third person narrative. The choice of a more distant narrator allows the author to view and present the events of the story with a greater sense of critical detachment.[2] Most of the drama in *La cosa buffa* occurs in the mind of the protagonist, and the actual events that take place in the story are of secondary importance as they serve only as a framework to his alienated thoughts.

Although the time of the novel is not given, precise references suggest that the story progresses from the end of October, 1939 until March 1940. Beyond the simple plot of *La cosa buffa* is a deep concern for man's isolation in modern society, and more specifically, for the alienation of man from woman. Olga Lombardi also sees Berto's love story as a symbol of man's difficult attempt to overcome his isolation and despair:

> A Berto non interessa tanto raccontare la storia d'amore tra Antonio e Maria quanto a rappresentare i caratteri, gli aspetti, i momenti di una situazione di pessimismo esistenziale, di inettitudine alle felicità, di fondamentale frustrazione.[3]

La cosa buffa picks up the thematic preoccupations of preceding novels and returns to a more traditional writing style, restoring punctuation and syntactical clarity. The title of the book, *La cosa buffa*, derives from one of three quotations which introduce the work. Berto uses an excerpt from Joseph Conrad to state the theme of his novel: "What a funny thing is life, such a mysterious articulation of unforgiving logic leading to a futile purpose." The second quote is from Henry Miller: "There is only a great adventure, that of the quest of inner reality, towards the "ego"; time, space, facts are so irrelevant." The third is from Musil: "We are, instead, at the mercy of the thing." Berto shares Conrad, Miller and Musil's disenchantment with life. Like them he is interested in exploring the subconscious, "la realtà interiore," and as in his earlier novels, existential despair, frustration, and guilt are the central concerns of this story of Antonio's isolation from others. But here humor —

---

[1] Giuseppe Berto, *La cosa buffa* (Milano: Rizzoli, 1966). All future references will appear parenthetically in the text as *CB*.

[2] For a more complete discussion see Lombardi, p. 73.

[3] Ibid., p. 78.

cockeyed, disquieting humor — is a most important aspect of the novel. It is through humor that Berto expresses his disturbing vision of life.

Berto unabashedly scrutinizes Antonio's alienation from women, his misunderstanding of their sexual needs. Some critics complain that his description of Antonio's clumsy and unfortunate attempts at love making is too graphic and indulgent. As Enrico Falqui, one of Berto's most outspoken critics, writes: "Qui [i punti scabrosi] sono anch'essi descritti fino all'ultima fibrilla, nonché fino allo scandalo, a piaceranno, oh se piaceranno, mentre in noi, lo confessiamo, hanno suscitato molta perplessità."[4] Berto defends himself against such accusations. He claims that he intended to describe the sexual inadequacies of a normal young male victim. According to him the hypocritical values of society and of the church are at fault. He:

> Devo attirare l'attenzione sulla circostanza che nè la famiglia, nè la scuola, nè la chiesa si vogliono assumere il compito dell'educazione sessuale dei giovani, e si limitano ad inculcare un innaturale sentimento sessuofobico.[5]

In fact, despite what some critics charge, in *La cosa buffa* Berto draws more than a picture of self-centered "love." Despite some explicit descriptions of sex, the author investigates alienation from others by emphasizing the relationship of man to woman. His scrutiny of the estrangement between the sexes focuses on Antonio's incapacity to relate to women and their sexual needs.

Antonio illustrates Berto's romantic concept of love. According to the author, love requires an understanding of sex and of religion. Only by overcoming the antagonistic and irrational feelings caused by an hypocritical religious education, which only apparently condemned the pleasures of physical love, may the protagonist be able to establish happy relationships with the opposite sex. Antonio, however, is inhibited by his idealistic unbringing. He is unable to free himself of the memory of a chaste mother who becomes a symbol of purity and innocence. He seeks in all women someone who can resemble his mother. *La cosa buffa* thus illustrates how the main source of conflict between a man and a woman stems from their different

---

[4] Falqui, quoted in Piancastelli, p. 97.
[5] Berto, quoted in Piancastelli, p. 97.

perceptions of love. More precisely, it centers on distinguishing between love and lust. Antonio seems unable to make this distinction; when he approaches women sexually he feels guilty and dirty, because he is obsessed with the memory of his mother, a submissive and romantic woman, a symbol of innocence and purity, and because he equates physical love with perversion.

The story is set in Venice, reminiscent of Berto's home. The story encompasses about four months, from November to March, in the life of its protagonist, Antonio. Like Berto, Antonio is a frustrated twenty-five year old elementary school teacher. He lives at home with a hostile father and a homely sister. His family alienates him. His father's expectations and violent outbursts push him more and more into a world of despair. To escape the stagnation of his home, Antonio lives isolated in his fantasies, in his thoughts of suicide, and also in his dreams to find the "anima gemmella," the girl of his dreams.

Antonio's description of Venice at the beginning of the novel conveys his alienation. He projects upon the landscape his mental anguish, making the city take on the somber contours of his mind:

> In quel tempo di mezzo inverno benché si recasse ogni pomeriggio di sole sulla terrazza del Caffè alle Zattere, vale a dire in un luogo per niente spiacevole e anzi rallegrato dalle scarse cose liete che si possono trovare in una città umida qual' è Venezia durante la brutta stagione, Antonio aveva soprattutto voglia di morire. Detto così il suo comportamento potrebbe benissimo apparire un po' scombinato e corrisponte ad uno stato psicologico quantomeno confuso. (CB, 9)

The city, symbolic of alienation, is the only place where Antonio can find refuge from the suffocation of his family environment. There, he can spend "ottocentonovantamila lire," about one thousand dollars, a modest amount, but he is convinced it is large enough to satisfy his cravings for something new and better in life. Finally, he thinks, he will be able to attract the attention of a woman. As a first step to this he buys himself a pair of shiny new shoes.

Aimlessly walking about Venice in the pale sunlight of November, absorbed in his confused blend of dark and happy thoughts, he arrives at the "Caffè delle zattere," where he first sees Maria. He recognizes her immediately as the girl of his dreams, the "anima gemella," and with Quixotic determination he approaches his Italian Dulcinea:

lf appresso proprio come un salame senza neanche il coraggio d'aprir bocca, *e se la faccenda dopo l'inizio tanto favorevole e promettente fosse andata a finire in nulla Antonio con ogni probabilità non avrebbe avuto da rimproverare che se stesso, e non sarebbe stata una bella cosa vista la sua già malferma fiducia nelle proprie capacità e il suo già più che sviluppato senso di colpa per la vita in generale.* (CB, 28)

To his disappointment, he discovers that Maria is the daughter of the Cavalier Ilario Borghetto, one of the richest men in Venice, an industrial magnate, owner of the shipbuilding company "Forniture Marittime Borghetto." Antonio makes a number of pretenses to hide his lowly social status, his poverty and especially the fact that he is a part-time school teacher; for instance, he tells her that, like herself, he is a university student, "fuori corso," hoping someday to become a famous writer.

Maria falls easy victim to Antonio's more experienced mannerisms and persuasive words. Unaware of his real shortcomings, she idealizes him and wants to give herself totally to him. Antonio, himself a victim of his distorted views, does not understand Maria's incipient sexual desires. His idealistic concept of love prevents it. Unable to accept a woman who is not a symbol of purity and innocence, he feels disgust at her surrender.

One day, however, he realizes that she can no longer continue to meet him in the dark corners of Venice. She decides to rent a room where they can be together undisturbed. After some misgivings on his part, Antonio is ready to take her virginity, when a frantic, violent knocking interrupts them. It is Mrs. Ilario Borghetto, Maria's mother. Antonio's reaction to this unexpected visit is typically ambiguous. On the one hand he is deeply shocked and afraid because he knows that he will lose forever his everlasting love, the "anima gemella"; on the other hand, he feels relieved that he has not tainted his love for Maria through sex (See CB, chapter X).

With the memory of Maria still too alive in his mind, and seeking also to escape his landlady's amorous attentions, Antonio leaves his apartment. Antonio's estrangement from reality is, in these circumstances, manifested by his absorption in the world of literature. He identifies with such romantic heroes as Foscolo's Jacopo Ortis or Goethe's Werther. Like them, he intends to immortalize and exhaust his love for Maria through an epistolary relationship, because he can no longer meet her (see CB, pp. 124-27). Proud of not having compromised his principles, he will not make a serious attempt to fight for her love. He is easily dissuaded by Maria's father and will readily accepts Signor Borghetto's payoff, promising never to see her again.

Antonio's unhappiness is nevertheless shortlived. Soon after losing Maria he meets Marica, a young Hungarian refugee who, unlike Maria, is shrewd, sensual, and bawdy. Antonio immediately sees in her a young woman needing his help and protection. It is the last day of "carnevale"; Antonio finds himself in the midst of the general euphoria. But his inner sadness keeps him isolated from the festivities all around him. Suddenly, a tall blond girl, attracted by his air of suffering, throws a handful of confetti at him. Antonio has the ominous premonition that this encounter will have a catastrophic effect on his life because, as he knows, Marica in Hungarian means "Maria."

Antonio is convinced that his encounter with Marica obeys a greater and mysterious force. Perhaps Marica is the necessary instrument which will enable him to expiate his wrongdoings to Maria. In any case, he seems determined not to waste any time in making her his. Consequently, he invites her to dinner and then to a hotel, where he makes love to her. Antonio is unaware of the frustration and disappointment his hastiness and his sexual impatience cause.

When Antonio wakes up he discovers that Marica has gone. The note she leaves on her pillow contains no explanations for such an abrupt departure. She only warns him against trying to look for her, although she promises that she will be in touch. Thus Antonio is left alone to contemplate his existential void, "L'inutilità e l'errore della propria esistenza" (CB, 268). Once again sex has contributed to his interpersonal alienation.

A week or more goes by without any news from Marica. This causes a great "infelicità esistenziale" in Antonio, who now doubts the value of living, to "procedere nella vita mettendo un po' più voglia di vivere nella molta voglia di morire" (CB, 280). Finally, he receives a letter from an anonymous "friend" including a long list of Marica's lovers. This information causes further distress, shame and guilt. Constantly wondering why his life is so unlucky, "abituali ragioni ch'egli aveva per sentirsi disgraziato" (CB, 290), he passes his days in Venice playing cards and drinking wine.

One cold and rainy night, Antonio has an unexpected surprise as he returns from Venice. He sees his "burbero padre" and "la triste sorella" happily in the company of a young blond girl, whom he immediately recognizes as Marica. The scene profoundly affects him. It is an unsual sight for him to see his father and sister engaged in a lively conversation, drinking the "grappa pregiata" usually reserved for the most special occasions. Antonio can only attribute this "clima di fastosa fratellanza" to Marica's "fascino," her charm, to the "astuzia," her shrewdness, of that "giovane avventuriera," the rogue from Budapest. Antonio, who has had nothing to eat all day long, chooses to wait outside "al freddo e all'umido." As he waits he has time to investigate the roots of his unhappiness and of his troubles. He can only remember that the few happy moments of his life were when his mother had been alive.

When Marica finally leaves the house, Antonio approaches her. Without saying a word he slaps her across the face. Only by resorting to violence does Antonio seem able to cope with his feelings of alienation:

> . . .egli sbucò all'improvviso dal nascondiglio e mentre lei non avendolo sul momento riconosciuto rimaneva sospesa e quasi sul punto di cacciare un urlo da dramma giallo egli la colpì con un violento schiaffo alla guancia destra chiamandola contemporaneament sgualdrina, e arrivato qui il nostro eroe aveva già del tutto acquisito il senso del ridicolo in cui s'era cacciato cioè aveva l'impressione di stare più che altro su di un palcoscenico a recitare La signora delle camelie o a cantare addirittura La traviata però capire d'essersi cacciato in un risibile imbroglio. (CB, 296-7)

Marica, after the initial pain, tells Antonio that she really loves him; knowing that he has behaved badly, he breaks down in apologetic tears. They leave, promising to see each other the next Saturday night at the "Magyar Hotel" where Marica is the night clerk. After sleepless nights Antonio goes to his rendezvous with the conviction that he will ask Marica to marry him; he does not imagine what is in store for him.

When he arrives at the hotel, Marica receives him with a warm smile. She has a room prepared for them on the top floor so that her jealous cousin Vera will not surprise them. She reveals that it was in fact Vera who wrote the letter full of lies about her "previous lovers" to Antonio because she was afraid that Marica might leave her. Later that night, when Marica and Antonio are together, Vera bursts into their room. The scene is infused with a sense of comedy and tragedy, "una scena da teatro lirico," (CB, 321) and closely parallels the episode of Mrs. Borghetto's intervention. Vera physically pulls Marica out of the room and convinces her that she cannot marry an indecisive, penniless individual like Antonio. Antonio's pride is as wounded, as it was when Maria's mother told him that her daughter deserved something better than a "maestro di campagna." Once again, displaying typical traits of alienated behavior, Antonio resorts to a grandiose act to protect himself against humiliation and defeat. He had shown his superiority to the Cavalier Borghetto by renouncing Maria; and now he lets Marica keep the expensive

71

engagement ring that he bought her with the last "centosettemila lire" of his grandfather's inheritance.

After Vera and Marica leave, Antonio is left alone to brood over his misfortunes and bad luck. Outside, the early morning approaches, and a thick fog envelops the city; again imagery which reflects the isolated and confusion of Antonio himself. This is the bitter end of a book that constantly oscillates between farce and tragedy. There seems to be little hope of Antonio overcoming his alienation. He has lost everything; his inheritance, his two lovers, his job, his respect for others. He truly seems on the verge of what Fromm calls the ultimate stage of alienation: insanity.

After a close reading of La cosa buffa it is possible to see that Antonio's story of his impossible loves is in essence an analysis of duality and ambiguity. This is reflected in both the characterization and the structure of the novel. Maria is a projection of Antonio's subconscious world. Like all of Berto's characters, she lacks definite physical characteristics; thus this description:

> . . .che Maria non fosse giustamente bella come a lui fin allora era parso e anzi che fosse piuttosto bruttina e che lui l'aveva vista bella solo perché l'aveva vista in una congiuntura molto particolare ossia quando un impellente necessità d'innamorarsi era capace di giocargli un brutto tiro a proposito della capacità di giudicare della bellezza femminile. (CB, 42)

The opposition with Marica is obvious. Maria is short and dark, Marica is tall and blond; one is a symbol of innocence, the other of sensuality. Yet Marica is Maria, in that they both represent extremes of a single personality — Antonio. They represent the two poles of his understanding of women. Because they are the product of his personality, one may observe that they are abstractions, and at the same time they embody Antonio's alienated self, the incarnation of his vacillating desires. This dualism, characteristic of Berto's novels, is seen in Il cielo è rosso (Carla/Giulia; Tullio/Daniele) and in Il brigante (Michele/Nino); it will also be manifest in Oh, Serafina (Augusto/Palmira) and La gloria (Judas/Christ). The pattern of rejection and guilt is complemented by constant repetitions of such words as "frustrazione, melanconia, colpa, morte, suicidio, pessimismo." Stream of consciousness and flashback also help to establish a sense of fragmented reality, of opposing states, of uncertainty.

Through humor, Berto penetrates the surface reality of things, and exposes the inner conflicts of his protagonist. However, some critics do not understand the function of humor in Berto. Thus Stephanie Harrington feels that the author's irony is detrimental to the novel. She explains: "There is something faintly disgusting in being made to look at young love through such very old eyes, by way of a narrator so sophisticated and worldy-wise."[6] The critic fails to see that Antonio and Marica and Maria are not true characters, but abstractions, projections of the author's own identity, symbols of Berto's alienated perception of existence.

In *La cosa buffa* Berto also reveals his concern for the craft of fiction. Through an effective use of stream of consciousness, Berto reveals the motivations and the background of his characters. He also uses flashbacks to give the reader the background information necessary to the understanding of both their psychological and social condition. He effectively employs the detached third person view to describe the protagonist's troubled state of mind, and he uses interior monologue to expose the workings of the protagonist's subconscious, providing an inward picture of his personal plight.

The humor is stylistically rendered by juxtaposing to Antonio's sad recollections of past events the contemplation of his problematic present and of bleaker days to come. The author depends on the participation of the reader's own perception of shared experiences. Hence, the humor entails two layers of awareness, one external, or grammatical, and one internal, or semantical. Our becoming amused derives not just from the grammatical incongruity, the intromission of colloquial expressions but entails also a semantical level which discloses a deeper truth. We are in fact amused in the recognition of the protagonist's own imperfection, his well deserved sense of inferiority. In a moment of despair he can only think about money. As Berto stated, the irony or sarcasm, if you will, is tempered though by our perception of his being cognizant of his personal deficiencies, his materialism and egocentricity. This is then the feeling of compassion that the author described as "pietas."

Oh, Serafina

With the publication of *Oh, Serafina*, by Rusconi in 1973, Berto continues his preoccupation with alienation.[7] To this point of his career, Berto had

[6] Stephanie Harrington, "Antonio in Love," *New York Times Book Review*, 20 October 1968, p. 55.

[7] Giuseppe Berto, *Oh! Serafina. Fiaba di ecologia, di manicomio e d'amore* (Milano: Rusconi, 1973). All future references will appear parenthetically in the text as *OS*.

dealt solely with the negative effects of personal and social estrangement. In this novel he emphasizes instead the positive aspects of alienation, namely the capacity of the individual to oppose and combat technological society.[8] Accordingly, Berto focuses on characters unable to relate to each other, and, particularly, on an individual whose madness places him in opposition to others. His efforts to protect his beliefs and to do away with the constraints of social conformity are the most important concerns of this novel.

As the author explains, he intended to write *Oh, Serafina* as a filmscript. In need of money, he hoped to resolve his financial situation by writing a successful screenplay:

> Ho scritto questo libro perché avevo bisogno di soldi. Mi capita spesso d'aver bisogno di soldi: non guadagno poi molto, sono imprevidente nelle spese, e lo Stato mi fa pagare troppe tasse. Di solito, risolvo questi problemi di denaro lavorando per il cinema. Anche questa volta volevo far così in effetti. *Oh, Serafina!* sarebbe dovuto essere soltanto un soggetto per film.[9]

The novel eventually was reworked into a film by Alberto Lattuada in 1974, and although it was awarded the "Premio Bancarella" the same year, it did not receive the same amount of critical attention bestowed on *Il male oscuro* and *La cosa buffa.*

While some critics agree that *Oh, Serafina* is truly a fable, as the subtitle *Favola di ecologia, di manicomio, e d'amore* indicates, others believe that the novel is a clear and bitter indictment of society. Carlo Bo calls the novel an "invective". Despite Berto's fundamental pessimism, Piancastelli sees a note of hope in the author's recognition of social ills. He calls it "a liberante fiaba dei nostri giorni." *Oh, Serafina* is indeed a "fable" for adults, which seems to invite the reader to reconsider the advantages of civilization.

The protagonist of the novel, thirty-three year old Augusto Secondo, inherits from his grandfather, a small factory, located in the outskirts of Milan. His great love for birds alienates him from his mother, then from his wife and finally from all those around him. The novel can be divided into two parts. The first part is set in "FIBA," the factory surrounded by a large and beautiful

---

[8]   See Armando Balduino, "Una 'fiaba di ecologia, di manicomio e d'amore di Giuseppe Berto," *Messaggi e problemi della letteratura contemporanea* (Venezia: Marsilio, 1976), pp. 133-135.

[9]   Berto, quoted in Lombardi, p. 95.

park, threatened by the expansion of the nearby industrial metropolis. The second part is set in the insane asylum, where Palmira (Augusto's wife), intending to rob him of his wealth, has isolated the simple-minded hero of the story. Though the novel is set in the present, the omniscient third person narrator goes back to 1920 to tell the story.

The novel begins with the formula of fairytales, "once upon a time there was . . ." a factory called FIBA "located just outside the city of Milan." It had been founded by Augusto Valle in 1920. Augusto Valle, like his grandson, was not interested in the success of his business, and instead spent most of his time flying over the countryside in his airplane. Ironically, one day in July 1944, the very object of Augusto's pleasure becomes the instrument of his death when he is killed in "Piazza Cordusio" during an air raid.

Augusto was as bizarre in death as he had been in life, naming as his only heir not his son, Giuseppe, but his four-year old grandson, Augusto Secondo. This move angered Augusto Secondo's mother, Belinda Sassi, a greedy and wicked woman, who thus began to harass her submissive husband to protest the will. Berto makes use of humor here when he plays on the names "Belinda Sassi in Valle": Belinda is in fact a ruinous landslide, "sassi," constantly falling upon the poor husband, the "valley."

The years go by, but the "fabbrichetta" and its surrounding park remain an island of green totally isolated from what is taking place around it. Augusto Secondo grows up unaware of what the world is truly like, oblivious to everything. He is, by nature, "malinconico" and "solitario." He communicates little with other people; he can only make friends with the birds of the park.

Belinda despises her son, and thinks him completely insane. One day, as she is observing him wholly absorbed in a conversation with his beloved birds, Belinda openly confronts Giuseppe and warns him that she is convinced that her son's behavior will drive her to madness, even to her tomb (OS, 11).

Belinda's constant nagging makes Giuseppe's life miserable. He lives in a state of torment. Finally, to everybody's suprise, he lives up to his threats of committing suicide. He climbs the church's steeple and from there he dives to his death. Belinda's scornful comment is as usual devoid of regrets: "L'hai voluta vinta tu" (OS, 14).

After his father's suicide Augusto assumes the direction of the company, while continuing his favorite activity, namely passing the afternoons conversing with the birds in the park. To everybody's surprise, Augusto Secondo, who by now is thirty-three years old, shows up promptly at work wearing an outfit that very closely recalls his grandfather's attire. At the sight of him, the old secretary, Rose, can barely breathe, and suppresses a scream of astonishment. When Belinda shows up with two workmen to remove the office picture of Augusto Valle, he firmly throws her out, using his most colorful Venetian dialect:

> "Donna, rompi no le bale. . . . Fuori di qui. Fuori."—La signora Belinda tentò di resistere.—"Che fai bastoni tu madre? Non temi il castigo di Dio?"
>
> "Fuori. A casa a fare la calza." (*OS*, 19)

Augusto Secondo is determined to leave everything unchanged, to continue to run things as his grandfather would have. Not only does he intend to keep his grandfather's picture in its place, but he also hangs up a picture of his father and a reproduction of Giotto's St. Francis of Assisi.

Meanwhile, the economic "boom" is threatening the factory and especially the park. The city is dangerously expanding towards the countryside, mother-of-pearl buttons are obsolete, plastic is lucrative. But Augusto fights his mother, the employees and everybody else to preserve the status quo. He refuses to improve his business in any way, insisting that his grandfather would not have approved; everything is to remain as if he were alive. Nothing must threaten the welfare of his trees and his birds.

Augusto falls in love with Palmira Radice, who works in the packing department. She is the sensual and shrewd sister of Romeo Radice, the foreman. No one approved of their marriage. The workers who know Palmira cannot understand why Augusto would want to marry "una puttana." Having no prior sexual experience, Augusto falls easily for the joys that Palmira can provide. He can finally understand why birds seem to have such a frenzied sexual activity.

During the honeymoon trip Augusto takes Palmira to Assisi's "basilica superiore" to see Giotto's portrait of his favorite saint preaching to the birds. There he falls into a state of profound admiration which his wife views with disgust. Returning to the factory, Augusto continues to ignore the course of his affairs, while spending more and more time conversing with his beloved birds. His disregard for his business now causes great concern even among the workers, who had previously liked his simple ways. Not even the arrival of a son, Giuseppe, detracts Augusto from the birds. He ignores the son, who, as Palmira tells him, has not been fathered by him but by one of his business competitors. Augusto now encounters the hostility of all, his entire family as well as his employees.

To convince him to sell the park and renovate the plant, Palmira withholds herself from his voracious sexual appetite. Deprived of sex, Augusto decides that his only joy in this life is his winged friends, hence he begins to identify more and more with St. Francis. Finally, with the help of the chief accountant and other important people, Palmira succeeds in having Augusto committed to the insane asylum. She claims that his bizarre love for birds not only prevented him from managing his business but also prevented him from behaving as a man and a father.

His confinement to the asylum begins a new life for Augusto. Despite the hardships typical of any seclusion which are made particularly painful for Augusto because he is forbidden any interaction with the few local birds, something unusually beautiful happens to him. Augusto meets Serafina, a young hippie with a very sad and painful past. She takes charge of his life and with her great passion guides him to a new life, filled with joy and hope.

Serafina is in the asylum because her father, an arrogant and powerful publisher, could no longer tolerate her open defiance. She broke all the family rules, she gave herself to any man, she led the workers against her father and helped them to organize their strikes. And when her father broke up her only true love relationship with Maurizio—an apparently inconclusive young man who wrote bad poetry and smoked much marijuana—she took revenge by abusing her body in any possible way she could. She even had four abortions, as she later confessed to Augusto.

The episode of the encounter between Serafina and Augusto is told with a blend of humor and lyricism. Augusto is in charge of the mail, and must deliver a postcard from India to Serafina. Not knowing her, he repeatedly asks the other inmates where she might be found. When he finds her, she is sitting cross-legged in deep mediation. Her blond silky hair is embellished with "lustrini e speccietti," and she wears the hippie uniform, "blue-jeans scampanati e sfrangiati," and bare feet. To Augusto's query, "Serafina Bozzoli," she auspiciously replies: "Ti aspettavo" (OS, 111).

Augusto has no doubt that she is "un angelo," his Beatrice, his future guide to a world of harmony and happiness:

"Sei tu Serafina Bòzzoli?"
    "Bozzòli", corresse mitemente, a alzò il viso.
Chiaro, incorniciato da biondi capelli a frangetta, quel viso era il viso più soave che si potesse immaginare, e gli occhi erano gli occhi più

puri che si potessero immaginare, con cielo dentro, e Augusto Secondo non fece alcuna fatica a paragonarla ad un angelo, anche perché a suo parere gli angeli, certo per via delle ali, erano la cosa più simile agli uccelli che ci fosse al mondo. (*OS*, 110)

As the subtitle promised, *Fiaba di ecologia, di manicomio, e d'amore*, the novel ends happily. Having promised her father that she will no longer misbehave, Serafina obtains a factory from him, the "Finca" (Spanish for "Farm"; it is perhaps Berto's ironic commentary on Mr. Bozzoli's fascist connections in South America), where they will be able to live. Augusto gives Palmira the rights to his factory and is also allowed to leave the hospital. At dawn Serafina and Augusto set off to the promised land south of Milan near Pavia. They leave on a cart pulled by oxen. On the wagon is a huge cage containing all the birds of the park; and accompanying them is the young Giuseppe and the old faithful Rosa, who had worked with Augusto's grandfather.

Their trip to Finca lasts four days and three nights, but the slowest part of their journey is spent trying to fight the heavy traffic of Milan. The bystanders do not know what to make of such a sight: some laugh, others applaud, a distinguished gentlemen with white hair and a white moustache removes his hat, a youngster tells his little girlfriend that they are part of Federico Barbarossa's army going to fight in the Holy Land—but she does not believe it.

They finally arrive at their destination before dawn. There is the Finca, a vast estate with green trees, inhabited by a great variety of birds. Augusto immediately releases the caged captives, who can now joyously fly in "un cielo più bello" (*OS*, 157). Serafina, Augusto, and the old and faithful signorina Rosa join hands in a cheerful dance of thanksgiving. They were, as the final sentence of the book states, "felici e contenti, e da allora in poi lo furono per sempre" (157). *Oh, Serafina*, then, is an allegory reminiscent of a Dantesque journey to paradise, a celebration of nature and freedom, and an outcry against the evil effects of today's technological society. It is both a fable and an "invective," recounting the fairytale life of Augusto, and indicting the society in which he can find no place.

As in the Berto's earlier works, the theme of alienation is accentuated and visualized by means of the setting and other symbols. For instance, the journey from FIBA to the Finca closely parallels that of Filippo Mangano in *Le opere di Dio*, in both novels there is a similarity in the biblical tone and description of the episodes. The journey is emblematic of the protagonists' uprootedness, of their separation from society and their quest for an identity.

Yet, the dance introduced at the end of *Oh, Serafina* can be interpreted as a celebration of freedom, as Augusto and Serafina rejoice in their break from familial and societal restraints.

The alienation caused by modern life is a most significant aspect of the novel, and is particularly evident in the antithesis of city and country. Life in the city is characterized by pollution, suffocation, decay and consequently death, whereas country life is pure, free and happy. Fog and rain are again associated with the city, as in the description of Milan: "il sole faceva quel che poteva per forare duecento metri di nebbia gravata da smog. Ci riusciva e non ci riusciva, a colpi d'aria si illuminava, e a colpi di di nuovo diventava cupa" (*OS*, 153). Once again, the city is a symbol of loneliness and despair. Berto despised living in cities and in fact chose like Augusto Secondo to live most of life in the self-imposed isolation of "Cape Vaticano," on the Calabrian Coast. In the following excerpt Berto sums up his assessment of the city as a disintegrating and dangerous world:

> La megalopoli, infatti, sempre più s'infettava, sempre più s'infittivano le ciminere eruttanti veleni foscamente colorati, sempre meno ci se vedeva, meno ci si respirava. I lombardi resistevano a tutte le lusinghe dei piani d'industrializzazione del Mezzogiorno, a tutti gli adescamenti del governo, a tutte le pressioni dei partiti politici, pur di starene lì, nella terra dove in fin dei conti erano nati, a metter su fabbriche, e quindi a polluire, come dicevano quelli che avevano visitato almeno una volta gli Stati Uniti (*OS*, 239).

Oh, Serafina thus illustrates the positive effects of alienation through Augusto's personal ordeals. His struggle against an hypocritical and materialistic society is a clear sign of how alienation can revitalize society, create new values and combat conformity. Erich Fromm explains that alienation can restore order and meaning in society provided that man "remains in touch with the fundamental facts of existence, if he can experience the exaltation of love and solidarity, as well as the tragic fact of his aloneness and of the fragmentary character of existence."[10]

Augusto strongly defends his individuality, or "madness," against family members and anybody else. He fights his own mother, driving her to her death (but she was so evil that this is in Augusto's favor), his wife, and his

---

[10] Fromm, *The Sane Society*, p. 83.

psychiatrist. What makes Augusto a true hero is that he represents the traditional "underdog" the lonely fighter against overwhelming odds. He speaks for all men against modern life and culture, and is truly heroic because he does not fall victim to it. Despite corrupting social forces, he remains pure and innocent.

Augusto's innocence can especially be seen in his understanding wholly different from Antonio in *La cosa buffa*. It is also different from his wife, Palmira's understanding, and this serves to alienate him from her. Berto seems to justify Augusto's lusty and almost animalistic sexual drive because he considers it primitive, natural, and consequently pure. Palmira's concept of love is conventional: she uses sex, as a practical instrument of power and exploitation, or something that can be bought and sold, a commodity. She embodies the twentieth century's concept of sex, which implies that women and men cannot enjoy a beautiful and complete relationship without an element of guilt or a feeling of dissatisfaction. Augusto's estrangement differs from other alienated characters because it does not derive only from his unhappy childhood; it is the result of his own nature.

Augusto Secondo shows greater inner strength; he is capable of dissenting constructively while opposing the annihilating forces of society. He gives up money and possessions to fight alone against technology and progress. Unlike those around him, he is integrated with nature; he seeks the real and rejects the artificial. He does not passively accept the judgments of others, especially those of the ruthless and dishonest. His integration with nature, shown by his love for his birds, shows that he is truly in touch with the essence of existence. Augusto's ultimate rejection of society becomes most evident in the end of the novel, when he actually builds a new society, the Finca, for himself and his family.

As in *La cosa buffa*, Berto uses humor to develop the theme of social alienation, a technique which allows him to give a running commentary upon the characters' thoughts and actions. It also accentuates the condemnation of social ills while decreasing its brutal impact on the reader. Humor does not, however, diminish Berto's keen perception of the real problems which are at the root of the book. On the cover page of *Oh, Serafina*, Berto explains that humor derives from his *pietas*, namely his knowledge of his own inadequacies and his compassion for others:

> Vi ho messo il mio 'humor' che ho imparato con lungo e duro lavoro, vi ho messo la mia 'pietas,' come direbbero i latini, cioè il mio rallegrarmi e allietarmi per ciò che mi sembra buono e il contristarmi per ciò che

mi sembra cattivo, e questa è cosa che ho imparato facilmente, a forza di sbagliare (*OS*, c.p.)

But beneath the comic facade of *Oh, Serafina* there lies a deep concern for death and the afterlife. Berto states: "Dei motivi che si trovano costanti nelle mie opere, qui manca solo, io credo, il senso della morte" (*OS*, c.p.). The author goes on to explain that the theme of death is absent from this work because, as in all fairy tales, the protagonists will live happily ever after, "questa è una favola, e i personaggi delle favole non hanno paura di morire perché, si sa, vivranno per sempre felici e contenti" (*OS*, c.p.).

It can be concluded that the alienation also has a positive aspect for Berto. Even if Berto in the novel juxtaposes fantasy and reality, its thrust remains the expression of individual freedom and imagination. It manifests the power of dissension through non-violence which is the only means to redefine values and goals for a better society.

La gloria

Published in Mondadori a few days before the author died in Rome on November 1, 1978, *La gloria* marks the end of Berto's literary production.[11] The most salient concerns of his previous works again prevail in this novel, namely the notion of the "male universale," the sense of guilt, the quest for God and literary glory. It is, much like *Male oscuro* and *Il cielo è rosso*, it is a book about Berto's personal anguish, his thoughts and his fears. Once again the author most intimately discloses his loneliness as a man and as an intellectual.

As critics have noted, *La gloria* is a sort of "testament," the ultimate spiritual legacy of Berto's embattled vision of self and life.[12] This autobiographical aspect of the novel is never hidden, for Berto clearly identifies himself with the protagonist and narrator of the novel, Judas. The parallel is confirmed by the author himself in an interview:

Ho sentitito il bisogno di scrivere il romanzo in prima persona per sot-

---

[11] Giuseppe Berto, *La gloria* (Milano: Mondadori, 1978). All future references to this work will appear parentically as *LG*.

[12] See Piancastelli, pp. 111-13.

81

tolineare questa identificazione con me. E' un libro sulla trascendenza. Io, come tanti non credo alla trascendenza ma ne sento il bisogno, ma nel mio primo libro dove pure la morte era presente sono riuscito a non scriver mai la parola anima per quattrocento pagine. [13]

Although the theme of guilt establishes a continuity between *La gloria* and the former works—Donald Heiney wrote that Judas is the "embodiment of guilt"—it is not the only concern of this work; moreover it is not exclusively the dominant concern in Berto. [14] Yet the majority of critics concentrate upon guilt, which they think resulted from Berto's unhappy relationship with his father, "la lunga lotta col padre." They neglect to examine the unity of Berto's "Weltanschauung," which includes themes of suffering, love, the isolation of man, and the struggle between father and son—all of which are symbols of his search for an integrated self, and of unification with God and society.

The central preoccupation of the book continues to be alienation. This time, however, Berto abandons humor, and replaces it with the subdued irony of his early works. As a result, the novel has a more lyrical tone, is filled with a sad and melancholy mood, better suited to the religious concern of *La gloria*.

Thus there is, once again, a successful conjunction of thematic concerns and structural devices. The theme of personal and interpersonal estrangement is reinforced by the fragmentation of the plot, character, and the symbolism of the setting.

The book begins with the depiction of Judea's political and social upheaval at the time of the arrival of Christ. Persecuted first by the Egyptians, then by the Babylonians, and now by the Romans, the Jews anxiously await the promised king who would lead them against the Romans and restore the unification and splendor they enjoyed during the reign of David. Judas speaks for all Jews when he calls upon God to hurry and send "Him," who could end the fratricidal dissent between the pharisees, scribes, and zealots. Their king Herod is a mad, bloodthirsty man. A puppet of the Romans, he does everything to maintain their trust, and is responsible for many bizarre acts of cruelty, including the massacre of thousands of children because he

---

[13] Giulia Massari, "La gloria," *Tuttolibri*, No. 41, 14 October, 1978, p. 4. See also Rossaná Ombres, "Sulle tracce di Giuda," *Tuttolibri*, No. 41, 11 November, 1978, p. 4.
[14] See Heiney, p. 238.

feared that one of them could have usurped his throne. In a fit of anger, he also killed his wife and two children with his own hands.

Corruption is everywhere; even the office of the high priest is commonly bought and sold. Judas can only blame God's silence for the Jews' plight: "Perché dormi, oh Signore? Perché la tua faccia distogli, la voce non fai sentire? Qual'è la colpa?" (LG, 9). These words introduce at the very beginning the existential themes the novel; man must withstand alone the evil and hardships of life which, as Judas interprets them, are an inexplicable punishment.

Judas is a strong, intelligent, impatient young man. When he first meets Christ he is in his early twenties. He happens to pass by the river where John the Baptist is about to baptize Jesus, and shares John's joy at recognizing the son of God: "Ecco l'angelo di Dio che toglie il peccato del mondo" (LG, 23). Judas is mysteriously attracted to Christ, but cannot explain to himself this irresistible call; the "incantamento," obliges him to rid himself of his fortune and to follow him.

However, Judas can never rid himself of his doubts about Christ's true identity. As he was suspicious of John the Baptist, so he is wary of Christ. Although always near whenever he performs his miracles or speaks to his many followers, Judas is not convinced; for him Jesus' marvelous accomplishments are little more than Egyptian magic. Judas also doubts Christ's intentions; in his view the acts are meant to dazzle the minds of the people. They are forms of propaganda to persuade them of his teachings, and not acts of love.

In a most important episode, Christ goes to Bethany to visit his friend Lazarus. Upon his arrival he finds Lazarus has been dead four days. Judas overhears Christ's conversation with Lazarus' sisters, Mary and Martha. Martha is in tears and seems to be scolding Christ for his delay: "Signore, se tu fossi arrivato in tempo questo non sarebbe successo" (LG, 118). Judas is indignant at Martha's requests, which he interprets as insolence. He is especially offended when Christ reassures her that Lazarus will be saved, and she replies, "Sì, il giorno del giudizio." Christ then asks to be taken to Lazarus's burial site. There he has the stone removed and calls forth his friend. To everyone's amazement, Lazarus appears at the entrance. For Judas this episode further proves Christ's incapacity to understand the real needs of his people. Why should he have performed miracles that had no political significance? Judas comments: "la ressurezione di Lazarus fu una ponderata, fredda, scenografica ciurmeria" (LG, 119). He seemed to do everything he could to violate the true teachings of the fathers. He taught love of one's enemies, and his humility implicitly encouraged weakness over strength. He exposed the hypocrisy of the priests and pharisees. In other words he seemed out of touch with the political reality of his times by not recognizing the Romans military power and the Jews' need of a strong leader. According to Judas, Christ should have been working for unity and power; instead he deepened the divisions among his people.

During Christ's visit to Lazarus, something also happens to deepen Judas's distrust: he rebukes Christ for having allowed Mary Magdalene to anoint his feet with a precious ointment that could have been sold for three hundred "denarii" to benefit the poor. John, Christ's favorite apostle, immediately intervenes to chastize Judas. Here the author shifts the narration to the third person and quotes directly from Luke's gospel. Then John explains that Judas is disappointed because as the Apostles' treasurer, he was in a position to steal from them. Indirectly, Jesus was giving away money that Judas could have had. However, Judas firmly denies these accusations. He claims that the other Apostles portray him unjustly. He was rich and had no need to steal.

As the book draws to its conclusion, Judas further describes the political confusion caused by Christ's rising popularity with the lower classes. After Christ's triumphant arrival in Jerusalem, Judas secretly meets in Aser's tavern with the leaders of the zealots, Ariel and Mahat. These fanatical opponents of the Romans are skeptical of Judas' request to help Christ's efforts. They question him on Christ's political views and intents. Does he have men willing to fight four thousand soldiers when assaulting the Roman fortress, "la Torre Antonia?" What kind of kingdom does he intend to establish? Would he be ready to fight alongside the allies of Rome, Egypt, and Syria? Judas cannot answer these questions. His frustration is augmented by his awareness of Christ's open disapproval and dislike for the Jewish establishment (LG, 128-30).

Suddenly, their meeting is disrupted by the arrival of a merchant, who loudly complains that something must be done about Christ. He then tells how Christ stormed into the temple, and like a madman furiously overturned tables, insulted the other merchants and bankers, and eventually chased everybody out. Others join in to berate Christ; they conclude that he was the cause of too much social disorder and disobedience. Finally, Judas can no longer endure the people's condemnation and speaks eloquently in Christ's defense. But when he leaves the tavern he realizes that Christ's cause is hopeless.

Filled with grief and guilt, he realizes that only an organized armed revolt led by the zealots can salvage the Jewish cause (LG, 131-37).

84

Judas seems aware that only in retrospect will the Jews learn from Christ's sacrifice. The guilt from his death will generate a new moral strength that will help them to achieve confidence as a unified people. In fact, the guilt for Christ's death contributed to generate a new faith and moral strength that helped the Jews achieve identity as a unified people. Judas is also aware that he is part of this destiny. Thus he understands that betrayal of Christ becomes a necessary condition for the future of the Jews and of humanity. So Judas meets Caiaphas and for thirty "denarii" assists in Christ's capture.

As Christ's life draws to an end so does Judas'. In the last pages of the book, Judas' confrontation with himself and with the meaning of his life reaches its climax. The spectacle of Christ's agony and his estrangement from all those who once said they loved him is too much for Judas to bear. In these last moments Judas finally becomes aware of Christ's true identity. It is his capacity to endure his isolation as a man, the silence of God, and the rejection of others that creates a bond between Judas and Christ. Soon Christ will die, and Judas will die also not far away by hanging himself on a fig tree. The same hand has determined their separate fates, and the two are united at last in death.

The end of the book is open to interpretation. It concludes with Christ's last words: "Dio mio, Dio mio, perché mi hai abbandonato?" (LG, 193). Christ's appeal to God speaks not only for Judas, but also for the author himself and for all of mankind.

Berto clearly does not intend to redeem the memory of Judas, one of the most wretched and despised figures in human history. He intends rather to portray the life of a man who, like himself, is searching for a meaning to existence. Judas' quest for himself, his problems in relating to his society, and his search for faith are intended by the author to inspire the minds of young people:

Il libro è stato prima di tutto utile a me, ma interesserà anche i giovani, perché tutta l'umanità ormai sa che il bene e il male coesistono. Il mio Gesù ha sentimenti poco generosi, per esempio verso il falegname Giuseppe e la vergine Maria; e il mio Giuda, in principio mosso da presunzione e da desiderio di gloria (per un attimo aveva creduto di essere lui l'unto del Signore.) è una vittima che alla fine implora, con le parole di chi sa, "non farmi soffrire più del giusto, Gesu, io la mia parte l'ho fatta. La storia l'abbandona al suo destino. L'opera si è compiuta, senza pieta.[15]

However, Berto intends this work to be more than a psychological study. *La gloria* is in fact reminiscent of *Il brigante*, which attempted to narrate a love story of political overtones. Like Michele Rende, Judas defends the rights of the lower classes against the rich and the powerful mixing Catholic with socialist beliefs. This does not prevent Berto from stating this stunch opposition to Marxism: "Io racconto una storia di duemila anni fa con i problemi di oggi. Cristo è l'unica forza che si contrappone al marxismo, è la civiltà occidentale contro quell'altra civiltà."[16] It is this unlikely ideological mixture, as Giorgio Barberi Squarotti points out, that is the weakest aspect of the book.

Neither politics nor theology, however, are the most important features of the book; truth, love, and identity are. *La gloria* is a story about the protagonist's embattled self. He is a troubled individual who displays traits of alienation as the protagonists of Berto's previous novels. Judas is torn by opposing feelings of love and hatred, jealousy and admiration for Christ. According to Horney, this emotional instability is characteristic of alienation. The individual becomes remote, indifferent, impersonal, and unable to recognize his true feelings. This is precisely what occurs in Judas' relationship with Jesus. Judas clearly displays neurotic symptoms that distort his perception of the Son of God. He projects his own personality upon Christ and thus begins a process of identification with him. Christ represents Judas' alter ego, or, in Freudian terms, "the ego ideal."

Judas' misunderstanding of Christ can be further explained in psychoanalytical terms. Laing, in *The Divided Self,* writes that the alienated individual provides himself with an identity by assuming the identity of another.[17] Hence, he projects his own personal characteristics upon another self and, at the same time, he identifies with the "other." Laing calls this "the false self system." The individual lives in a state of self-deception which can easily be described as "mauvaise fois," to use Sartre's term. Unable to have a "real" perception of himself, the alienated man sees himself as an empty mark, a puppet of others, without a grasp on his existence. He copes with his feelings of rejection and isolation by further distancing himself from others. Social interaction can only confirm his negative perception of himself and of others.

---

15 Berto, quoted in Massari, p. 4.
16 Berto, quoted in Massari, p. 4.
17 See R.D. Laing, *The Divided Self* (Harmondsworth, Middlesex: Penguin Books, 1973), pp. 65-120.

He is a victim first of himself and then of external pressures. Withdrawn in the gloomy sphere of his private self, he neither perceives nor understands what others feel, and this generates an unrelenting sense of guilt which he disguises by assuming an arrogant, seemingly unfeeling demeanor.[18]

---

[18] Johnson, *Alienation: Concept, Term and Meanings*, p. 303.

Conclusion

In the preface to *Il brigante* Giuseppe Berto wrote that his narrative constitutes a "letteratura d'alienazione." The present study has attempted to show that characters' mental anguish, their quest for a sense of identity and their pursuit of God, exhibits three types of alienation, namely from God, from self and from others; thus alienation is the cohesive principle unifying Berto's apparently disparate literary corpus. It has been shown also that the roots of alienation are in religious, familial, personal, and social conflicts. Not only is it manifest in the relationships between the characters, but it permeates all aspects of his novels; the plot, setting, and style. In fact, the most important stylistic device to underscore the theme of alienation is Berto's use of stream of consciousness. Through this technique the author can manipulate space and time by internalizing the action. The story must then unfold according to the protagonist's erratic mental associations.

Like Kierkegaard, Sartre, and Camus, Berto's novels confront the riddles of human psyche and of life. From his perspective, the frustration, loneliness and guilt afflicting the protagonists of his novels are the result of a mysterious disease, "il male universale," a cosmic evil power which pervades the whole of mankind. His characters thus are metaphorical representations of man's predicament. Having lost their moral and mental equilibrium through unfortunate experiences, they live in constant struggles to regain it.

In search of selfhood and of a transcedent reality, the characters face the dread of existential nothingness and death. They are unhappy, ridden with guilt, incapable of establishing positive relationships with others, clearly displaying the symptoms of alienation, they withdraw into a private world of fantasy and despair. One can follow the development of this alienation in a clear pattern: first there is an unhappy childhood due to the presence of a domineering father and a submissive mother, then the horror and humiliation of war and imprisonment, and finally a rejection by society. What really makes these figures true to life is Berto's poignant portrayal of their states of mind. Daniele, Michele Rende, Antonio, Augusto Secondo and even Judas are all projections of Berto's self. Like the author, they are victims of their own insecurities; outcasts and loners who struggle to gain an understanding of the presence of evil and suffering in the world. They accurately reflect the author's philosophy of life as well as his vision of the life of the afflicted and the downcast.

If we compare the earlier works with his later ones, it is possible to see a pattern of development in Berto's fiction. In the early neorealist fiction alienation is a state into which men are born and from which they cannot emerge. The protagonists see God as responsible for their precarious existence because of his silence and indifference. They are victims of the "male universale." Unable to comprehend the evil that is afflicting them, these characters take shelter from life in the consumption of alcohol as Filippo Mangano in *Le opere di Dio*; they become outlaws as Michele Rende in *Il brigante*; they commit suicide as Daniele in *Il cielo è rosso*. Their distorted perspectives allows them to relate to life only by means of a desperate, irrational and antisocial attempt. But in *Il male oscuro*, *La cosa buffa*, *Oh, Serafina!*, and particularly, *La gloria*, the protagonists seem able to gain their inner equilibrium, struggling, as they are, to cope and to understand the causes and manifestations of their troubled realities.

These novels unfold in an atmosphere of death, void, anger and sensuality. The spiritual and physical misery of the characters is conveyed through various symbols. "The city of the dead," the magnolia tree, rain, fog, and cold are part of a hostile, natural setting emblematic of their plight. Alienation is also represented symbolically by the contrast between dark and light, city and country, sanity and insanity and other images connoting confinement and fragmentation. On the other hand, Berto uses images of birds and flight to underscore freedom and happiness.

Berto also uses humor to achieve his aims; as he explained: "All' umorismo credo di essere arrivato perché è l'unica via di sfuggire alla nevrosi." Through irony the author views and exposes the fears and insecurities of the protagonists while assuming a critical distance from them and from himself.

As the parallel with Albert Camus has indicated, humor has a philosophical significance. It expresses the writer's belief that man must attempt, through laughter, to gain control over the threatening forces of the world.

Hence, it can be observed that humor is both the external symptom of alienation as well as a relief.

Berto's emphasis on the psychological disturbances manifested by his
characters distinguishes him from most of his contemporaries such as Vittori-
ni, Pavese, Silone and Levi who aspired to a "letteratura impegnata"—a tes-
timony to the political ills of contemporary Italian society. Berto avoided a
detailed analysis of Italian life, politics, religion and the economy. He focused
on universal themes with an emphasis on feelings or states of mind more
than ideas.

Berto's fiction despite the opinions of some critics, has received vast
public acclaim in Italy and abroad. This must be attributed to his capacity to
deal convincingly with themes of universal interest. In his writing Berto com-
bines comedy with lyricism to portray perceptively the disenchantment and
frustration modern man faces in a seemingly evil society. His concern as a
writer does not focus on specific political or social issues, rather it investigates
the human condition. Despite what appears to be a lack of coherent political
ideology, his romantic attempt to fuse Marxism and Catholicism, Berto de-
serves greater critical recognition. His name is still not included in many surveys of contemporary literature. Yet Berto is not a minor writer.

His concern for man's isolation and mental anguish should place his fiction within the mainstream of contemporary literary trends. Like Sartre, Camus, Hemingway, Carlos Fuentes, Saul Bellow, and so diverse Italian writers
such as Gadda, Buzzati, Mastronardi, Landolfi, Moravia Berto seeks an
answer to life's riddles and to man's estranged state in society. His books,
therefore, deserve greater recognition due to their exploration of one of the
essential themes of twentieth century. Berto's own assessment of his work
contained in *L'inconsapevole approccio* is an appropriate conclusion to this
study:

> Il Nostro [Berto], a costo di pensarla diversamente dall'imperituro Be-
> nedetto Croce, crede che il linguaggio sia un fatto morale più che este-
> tico, e che la letteratura sia comunque vita, anche vita di sé con gli altri
> (101).

Selected Bibliography

I. WORKS BY GIUSEPPE BERTO

La colonna Feletti (short story) Venezia, "Gazzettino Sera", 17, 18, 21, 24 September 1940.

Il cielo è rosso (novel, original title: *La perduta gente*), Milano, Longanesi, 1947, 1954; Milano, Rizzoli, 1969.

Le opere di Dio (novel), Roma, Macchia, 1948 (reprinted with the addition of a long essay, *L'inconsapevole approccio*, Milano, Nuova Accademia, 1965).

Il brigante (novel), Torino, Einaudi, 1951; Milano, Longanesi, 1961; Milano, Rusconi, 1974.

Guerra in camicia nera (novel), Milano, Longanesi, 1955, 1969.

Un po' di successo (short stories), Milano, Longanesi, 1963.

L'uomo e la sua morte (play), Brescia, Morcelliana, 1964.

Il male oscuro (novel), Milano, Rizzoli, 1964.

La fantarca (science fiction fable), Milano, Rizzoli, 1965.

La cosa buffa (novel), Milano, Rizzoli, 1966.

Modesta proposta per prevenire (essay), Milano, Rizzoli, 1971.

Anonimo veneziano (screenplay), Milano, Rizzoli, 1971.

La Passione secondo noi stessi (play), Milano, Rizzoli, 1972.

Oh, Serafina! (novel), Milano, Rusconi, 1973.

È forse amore (short stories), Milano, Rusconi, 1975.

Anonimo Veneziano (novel), Milano, Rizzoli, 1976.

La gloria (novel), Milano: Mondadori, 1978.

II. TRANSLATIONS OF BERTO'S WORKS

Antonio in Love. Trans. William Weaver (New York: Knopf, 1968) (trans. of
  La cosa buffa)
The Brigand. Trans. August Davidson (New York: New Directions, 1951)
  (trans. of *Il brigante*)
Il cielo está rojo. Trans. A. Gregori (Mexico: Jackson, 1950).
Incubus. Trans. William Weaver (New York: A.A. Knopf, 1066) (trans. of *Il
  male oscuro*)
The Sky is Red. Trans. Angus Davidson (New York: New Directions, 1948).
The Works of God and Other Stories. Trans. Angus Davidson (Norfolk,
  Conn.: New Directions, 1950) (trans. of *Le opere di Dio*).

III. WORKS CONSULTED

Baker, Charles. *Hemingway: The Writer as Artist*. Princeton, New Jersey:
  Princeton University Press, 1963.
Balduino, Arnando. "Una fiaba di ecologia, di manicomio e d'amore" di
  Giuseppe Berto, *Messaggi e problemi della letteratura contempora-
  nea*. Venezia: Marsilio, 1976, 133-45.
Barberi Squarotti, Giorgio. *Poesie e narrative del secondo novecento*. Mila-
  no: Mursia, 1978.
Barberi Squarotti, Giorgio. *La narrativa italiana dopoguerra*. Rocca San Cas-
  ciano: Cappelli, 1965.
Bier, William. *Alienation: Plight of Modern Man?*. New York: Fordham Uni-
  versity Press, 1972.
Bloom, Harold. *The Anxiety of Influences*. New York: Oxford University
  Press, 1973.
Booth, Wayne C. *A Rhetoric of Fiction*. Chicago: The University of Chicago
  Press, 1961.
Booth, Wayne C. *A Rhetoric of Irony*. Chicago: The University of Chicago
  Press, 1975.
Camus, Albert. *The Myth of Sisyphus and Other Essays*, trans. Justin
  O'Brien, New York: A.A. Knopf, 1955.
Camus, Albert. *Le Mythe de Sisyphe*. Paris: Gallimard, 1942.
Camus, Albert. *The Stranger*. trans. Kate Griffith, Washington: University
  Press of America, 1982.

Coles, Robert. "Anaylsis Italian Style" *The New Republic*, 16 July, 1966, pp. 23-25.

Curley, Arthur. "Antonio in Love" *Library Journal*, No. 93, 1 November, 1968, p. 4164.

D'Agostino, Vincenzo. *Civiltà letteraria del Novecento.* Catanzaro: Edizioni Frama Sud, 1980.

Davis, R.M. *The Novel: Modern Essays in Criticism.* Englewood Cliffs: Prentice Hall, 1969.

Diagnostic and Statistical Manual of Mental Disorders. 2nd edition, Washington, D.C.: American Psychiatric Association, 1968.

Dizionario Motta della letteratura contemporanea. ed. Federico Motta, Milano, 1980.

Dizionario Della Letteratura Mondiale del 900. ed. Francesco Licino Galati, Roma: Edizioni Paoline, 1980.

Eco, Umberto. *Semiotics and the Philosophy of Language.* Bloomington Indiana University Press, 1984.

Encyclopedia of Mental Health. ed. Albert Deutsch, Metuchen, N.J.: Mini Print Co., 1970.

Enright, D.J. "Antonio in Love" *New York Review of Books*, 21 November, 1968.

Esposito, Rossana. "Rassegna di studi su Giuseppe Berto," *Critica Letteraria.* 1 (1973) 176-84.

Esslin, Martin. *The Theatre of the Absurd.* Harmondsworth: Penguin Books, 1968.

Fabiani, Enzo. "Berto" *Gente*, 28 September, 1978, pp. 173-76.

Falqui, Enrico. *Novecento Letterario.* Firenze: Vallecchi, 1961.

Feinberg, Leonard. *The Secret of Humor.* Amsterdam: Rodopi, 1978.

Ferguson, George. *Signs and Symbols in Christian Art.* London: Oxford University Press, 1973.

Finfter, Ada W. ed. *Alienation and the Social System.* New York: John Wiley and Sons, Inc., 1972.

Fromm, Erich. *The Sane Society.* New York: Holt, Rinehart and Winston, 1955.

Frye, Northrop. "The Four Forms of Fiction," *Hudson Review*, 2 (Winter, 1950), 582-599.

Freud, Sigmund. "Some Character Types Met in Psychoanalytical Work," *The Standard Edition of the Complete Psychological Works of Sigmund Freud.* Vol. 14, trans. and ed. J. Strachey, London: Hogarth Press, 309-333.

Gross, John. "The Sky is Red," *The Christian Science Monitor*. 30 September, 1948, pp. 11-12.

Handlin, Oscar. "Incubus," *Atlantic Monthly*. 217, March 1965, pp. 162-64.

Harrington, Stephanie. "Prisoned in the Self," *New York Times Book Review*. 20 October, 1968, p. 55.

Hayes, Alfred. "The Works of God," *New York Herald Tribune*. 18 June, 1950, p. 26.

Heiney, Donald. *America in Modern Italian Literature*. New Brunswick: Rutgers University Press, 1964.

Heiney, Donald. "The Final Glory of Giuseppe Berto," *World Literature Today*, 54 (1980), 238-40.

Hemingway, Ernest. *The Short Stories of Ernest Hemingway*. New York: Charles Scribner's Sons, 1938.

Hemingway, Ernest. *The Old Man and the Sea*. New York: Charles Scribner's Sons, 1953.

Johnson, Frank, ed. *Alienation: Concept, Term, and Meanings*. New York: Seminar Press, 1973.

Jung, Carl C. *Psychological Types*. trans. R.F.D. Hull, Princeton: Princeton University Press, 1971.

Kierkegaard, Sören. *Concluding Unscientific Postscript*, trans. Swenson, Princeton, N.J.: Princeton University Press, 1944.

Laing, R.D. *The Divided Self*. Harmondsworth, Middlesex: Pengiun Books, 1973.

Lanapoppi, Aleramo P. "Immanenza e trascendenza nell'opera di Giuseppe Berto: "la trappola del neorealismo," *Modern Language Notes*, 85, 1 (January 1, 1970), 42-66.

Lanapoppi, Aleramo P. "Immanenza e trascendenza nell'opera di Giuseppe Berto:) La realtà di dentro." *Modern Language Notes*. 87, 1 (January 1972), 78-104.

Leone, Michele. *L'industria nella letteratura italiana contemporanea*. Saratoga, CA: Anma Libri, 1976.

Lombardi, Olga. *Invito alla lettura di Giuseppe Berto*. Milano: Mursia, 1974.

Manacorda, Giuliano. *Vent'anni di pazienza*. Firenze: La Nuova Italia, 1972. 1972.

Marabini, Claudio. *Gli anni sessanta: narrativa e storia*. Milano: Rizzoli, 1969.

Marcuse, Herbert. *Reason and Revolution: Hegel and the Rise of Social Theory*. New York: Oxford University Press, 1941.

Maschio, Giovanni Battista. *Panorama letterario del Novecento*. Torino: Paravia, 1971.

Massari, Giulia. "La gloria," *Tuttolibri*, No. 41, 14 October 1978, p. 4.

Mazzolana, Bruna Baldini. *Alberto Moravia e l'alienazione*. Milano: Ceschina, 1971.

Mindness, Harvey. *Laughter and Liberation*. Los Angeles: Nash, 1971.

Molina, Fernando. *Existentialism as Philosophy*. Englewood Cliff, N.J.: Prentice Hall, 1962.

Montanelli, Inoro "Il male oscuro," *Corriere della Sera*. 8 April, 1964, p. 7.

Monterosso, Ferruccio. *Come leggere il Male Oscuro di Giuseppe Berto*. Milano: Mursia, 1977.

Moravia, Alberto. *L'uomo come fine e altri saggi*. Milano: Bompiani, 1964.

Murphy, Carol J. *Alienation and Absence in the Novels of Marguerite Duras*. Lexington, Kentucky: French Forum Publishers, 1982.

Ombres, Rossana. "Sulle tracce di Giuda." *Tuttolibri*. No. 41, (11 November, 1978), p. 4.

Pacifici, Sergio. *A Guide to Contemporary Italian Literature*. Cleveland: The World Publishing Company, 1962.

Pancrazi, Pietro. *Scrittori d'oggi*. Bari: Laterza, 1950.

Piancastelli, Corrado. *Berto*. Firenze: La Nuova Italia, 1970.

Piancastelli, Corrado. "Berto," *Novecento*. ed. Gianni Grana, Milano: Marzorati, 1979, Vol. ix, pp. 7866-86.

Pirandello, Luigi. *On Humor*. Antonio Illiano and Daniel P. Testa, ed., Chapel Hill, The University of North Carolina Press, 1960.

Poggioli, Renato. *The Theory of the Avante-Garde*, trans. Fitzgerald, Cambridge: Harvard University Press, 1968.

Pullini, Giorgio. "Berto", *Novecento*, ed. Gianni Grana. Milano: Marzoriati, 1979. Vol. ix, 7887-91.

Pullini, Giorgio. *Il romanzo italiano del dopoguerra*. Padova: Marsilio, 1965.

Pullini, Giorgio. *Volti e risvolti del romanzo italiano contemporaneo*. Milano: Mursia, 1971.

Robbe-Grillet, Alain. *For a new novel*. New York: Grove, 1965.

Samstag, Nicholas. "Incubus," *Saturday Review* 49, March 12, 1966.

Schafer, Roy. "The Pursuit of Failure and the Idealization of Unhappiness," *American Psychologist*. April 4, 1984. pp. 16-17.

Schacht, Richard. *Alienation*. Garden City, New Jersey: Doubleday, 1970.

Storia della letteratura italiana. "Il Novecento," Milano: Garzanti, 1969.

Sykes, Gerald. *Alienation: The Cultural Climate of our Time*. New York: George Brazilier, 1964.

Sypher, Wylie. *Loss of the Self in Modern Literature and Art*. New York: Random House, 1962.

Thody, Philip. "A note on Camus and the American Novel," *Comparative Literature*, 9 (Summer, 1957), 249-57.

Ullman, Stephen. *Style in the French Novel*. Oxford: Oxford University Press, 1964.

Young, Philip. *Ernest Hemingway: The Writer as Artist*. Princeton, New Jersey: Princeton University Press, 1963.

Scripta humanistica

Directed by
BRUNO M. DAMIANI
The Catholic University of America
COMPREHENSIVE LIST OF PUBLICATIONS *

18. *Estudios literarios en honor de Gustavo Correa.* Eds. Charles Faulhaber, Richard Kinkade, T.A. Perry. Preface by Manuel Durán. $25.00
19. George Yost, *Pieracci and Shelly: An Italian Ur-Cenci.* $27.50
20. Zelda Irene Brooks, *The Poetry of Gabriel Celaya.* $26.00
21. *La relación o naufragios de Alvar Núñez Cabeza de Vaca,* eds. Martin A. Favata y José B. Fernández. $27.50
22. Pamela S. Brakhage, *The Theology of «La Lozana andaluza.»* $27.50
23. Jorge Checa, *Gracián y la imaginación arquitectónica.* $28.00
24. Gloria Gálvez Lira, *Maria Luisa Bombal: Realidad y Fantasía.* $28.50
25. Susana Hernández Araico, *Ironía y tragedia en Calderón.* $25.00
26. Philip J. Spartano, *Giacomo Zanella: Poet, Essayist, and Critic of the «Risorgimento.»* Preface by Roberto Severino. $24.00
27. E. Kate Stewart, *Arthur Sherburne Hardy: Man of American Letters.* Preface by Louis Budd. $28.50
28. Giovanni Boccaccio, *The Decameron.* English Adaptation by Carmelo Gariano. $30.00
29. Giacomo A. Striuli, *«Alienation in Giuseppe Berto».* $26.50
30. Barbara Mujica, *Iberian Pastoral Characters.* Preface by Frederick A. de Armas. $33.00
31. Susan Niehoff McCrary, *«'El último godo' and the Dynamics of the Urdrama,»* Preface by John E. Keller. $27.50

Forthcoming

* Carlo Di Maio, *Antifeminism in Selected Works of Enrique Jardiel Poncela.* $20.50
* Juan de Mena, *Coplas de los siete pecados mortales: Second and Third Continuations.* Ed. Gladys Rivera. $25.50
* Francisco Delicado, *Portrait of Lozana: The Exuberant Andalusian Woman.* Translation, introduction and notes by Bruno M. Damiani. $33.00
* Salvatore Calomino, *From Verse to Prose: The Barlaam and Josaphat Legend in Fifteenth-Century Germany.* $28.00
* Darlene Lorenz-González, *A Phonemic Description of the Andalusian Dialect Spoken in Almogía, Málaga — Spain.* $25.00
* Maricel Presilla, *The Politics of Death in the «Cantigas de Santa María.»* Preface by John E. Keller. Introduction by Norman F. Cantor. $27.50
* *Studies in Honor of Elias Rivers,* eds. Bruno M. Damiani and Ruth El Saffar. $25.00

BOOK ORDERS

* Clothbound. *All book orders,* except library orders, must be prepaid and addressed to **Scripta Humanistica**, 1383 Kersey Lane, Potomac, Maryland 20854. *Manuscripts* to be considered for publication should be sent to the same address.

www.ingramcontent.com/pod-product-compliance
Lightning Source LLC
Chambersburg PA
CBHW020809100426
42814CB00001B/3